CAREER TESTS

CAREER TESTS

25 REVEALING SELF-TESTS TO HELP YOU FIND AND SUCCEED AT THE PERFECT CAREER

Louis Janda, Ph.D.

BARNES
&NOBLE
BOOKS

NEW YORK

2004 Barnes & Noble Books

ISBN 0-7607-6765-3

Printed and bound in the United States of America

04 05 06 07 08 09 MC 9 8 7 6 5 4 3 2 1

For Rick Balkin,
my agent and friend,
who helped me make an adjustment in my
career direction

Contents

Part III: Room for Improvement 67

Part IV: Being Prepared for the Right Job 111

Introduction

I believe that career opportunities are greater today than ever before. That is quite a sweeping statement, especially coming from someone with so little knowledge of history, but the evidence seems overwhelming to me. One of my grandfathers, who could only be described as artistic, had the ability to make things from ordinary boards, yet he was grateful that he could provide his family with a modest home, impossibly small by today's standards. My other grandfather worked from sunup to sundown on the family farm, yet buying new shoes for his children was a momentous occasion. Both men were intelligent, skilled, and hardworking, but they never dreamed it might be possible to retire early and spend their later years in the sunbelt, lounging by the pool or meeting friends on the first tee for a leisurely round of golf.

Today, as the twentieth century is coming to a close, I have a cousin who followed my maternal side of the family's farming tradition, and he recently bought an airplane because he had the urge to try something new. A few months ago, my wife, Meredith, and I were planning to have some remodeling work done on our house, and we could not find a carpenter (forget an artist with wood) who was willing to work for less than $40 per hour—considerably more than I make as a college professor. I have a number of friends who own small businesses—paint contracting, lawn irrigation, and carpet installation, to name just a few—who do well enough to drive Volvos and play golf at their country clubs on the weekends. There is no doubt in my mind that people who are determined to succeed and who are willing to work hard have virtually unlimited opportunities today.

So what distinguishes those who have successful and gratifying careers from those who never seem to get ahead and who hate their jobs? Successful people have the desire to make it. They want to be proficient at their work not only for the financial rewards but also, and perhaps more importantly, for the evidence that they are good at what they do. Those who seem to flounder throughout their careers see their jobs merely as work. They have to do it to survive, but they derive little pleasure from doing it well. Their only goal is to make it to the weekend or the next vacation, when they can have a brief respite from such an onerous activity.

If you are reading these words, I am willing to bet you share the characteristics of successful people. Clearly, you care about your career and want it to be more than a job, more than a means of subsistence. Do not minimize this quality. Without it, you do not have much of a chance to succeed. With it, the only way you can fail is if you give up.

Also, successful people know what they want from life and are unwilling to settle for less. Too many people, once they realize the time has come for them to earn a living, settle for the first decent job that comes along even if they cannot generate any enthusiasm for it. It should come as no surprise that these are the people who, ten to twenty years later, spend their workdays counting the hours to the weekend. There is no reason to settle for so little. Regardless of your interests, you can find a career that allows you to express them. It is crucial, however, that you take an active role in determining your career path. If you take the course of least resistance and accept the first offer you receive, you increase the odds that your career will result in frustration and a sense of drudgery.

My goal in preparing this collection of tests is to provide you with a sense of direction in your search for the right career. I have divided the tests into four sections. Part I, "Getting Started," provides a series of tests to measure your vocational maturity and interests. These tests were designed for young adults and will help you focus your thoughts so that you can get your career search off to a good start. If you are a student, you will definitely want to take these tests first. They will also be useful for those who are currently employed but did not follow a well-thought-out plan to obtain their present jobs.

The tests in Part II, "Evaluating Where You Are Now," are for people who are currently employed. Some people are fortunate in that they know they love everything about their jobs. Others have no uncertainty about hating everything about their jobs. But most of us fall somewhere between these two extremes. We enjoy some aspects of our jobs, but we find other aspects unpleasant or stressful. The tests in this section will give you the opportunity to discover how your feelings about your job compare with those of other people. If you are not currently employed, use your favorite past job as a frame of reference. You may learn that it is possible to find more gratifying work.

The tests in Part III, "Room for Improvement," includes tests that are related to success. Clearly, successful people recognize their strengths and weaknesses. They capitalize on their strengths, and if their weaknesses get in the way, they make the necessary effort to change. The tests in this section will help you to identify your strong points as well as those areas that could stand some improvement. I will provide a few hints after each test as to how you can deal effectively with any weaknesses you discover.

The tests in Part IV, "Being Prepared for the Right Job," include tests to help you learn how to present yourself more effectively for that job you want. The first two tests in this section, the "Assertive Job Hunting Survey" and the "Job Interview Self-Statement Schedule," will identify any areas you might need to work on in order to get that all-important job offer. The remaining seven tests in this section are quite similar to tests actually used by potential employers. They will help you to sharpen your test-taking skills and provide you with useful information about the types of careers you are most likely to find satisfying.

A majority of the tests in this book can be viewed as personality tests. Researchers have discovered that people who experience a good fit between their personality style and the demands of their job have greater job satisfaction, career stability, and career success. Dr. John Holland, a psychologist who has devoted his career to this topic, concluded that there is a very close connection between personality and vocational interests. Perhaps one of the more intriguing findings of his research is that our vocational interests have much broader implications than simply what career path we are likely to pursue. For instance, college roommates who have different vocational interests are less likely to get along than are roommates with similar

interests. When men and women divorce and remarry, their second spouse is likely to have vocational interests more similar to their own than did the first spouse. And clients tend to believe that their counselors are more helpful when they share similar vocational interests.

Holland has also argued that there is a close connection between our personality style and our aptitudes. For example, "Realistic" personality types are likely to have the ability to manipulate machines and tools. Depending on the level of ability and motivation of people of this type, they tend to settle in occupations such as carpenter, electrician, or mechanical engineer. As a second example, "Enterprising" types have the ability to persuade, manipulate, or direct other people. Typical occupations for these people include retail manager and lawyer.

The important implication of Holland's research is that we tend to gravitate to and be interested in areas that are consistent with our personalities. So, Realistic people are likely to acquire the skills that allow them to manipulate machines and tools, and Enterprising types learn what they need to know to be persuasive and effective managers. This means that the measurement of specific aptitudes is not nearly as important in helping people find an appropriate career path as is the measurement of personality characteristics. Thus, the myriad aptitude tests that were so popular during the middle part of this century have fallen into disfavor, to be replaced with tests similar to those found in this book. As Holland has convincingly argued, the key to having a satisfying, stable, and successful career is to find a job that is a good match with your personality.

A Few Words about the Tests in This Book

Career testing is big business. Every year, millions of high school and college students take psychological tests to help them bring their plans for a career into focus. Estimates are that two thirds of all employers use tests to select among job applicants. Furthermore, more than two thousand occupations, ranging from real estate agent to psychologist, require that individuals pass a test for licensure or certification. Career testing is a billion dollar industry.

Because career testing is such a lucrative business, the publishers of these tests are not about to let me reproduce their instruments here. So, the tests you will find in the following pages, although not used commercially, are very similar to those that are. A majority of them were developed by university research psychologists as tools to help them learn more about employee selection and career development. This does not mean that they are not as good as the tests that cost anywhere from $15 to $100 per person to take. The authors of tests face the same hurdles that all creative people do. Perhaps the publisher did not see a substantial market for the new test. Perhaps it was viewed as being too much like an existing test. Or while it may have offered an improvement over an existing test, it may not have been seen as offering enough of a

difference to compete successfully with older, established tests. The point is that there are many excellent tests that have never made it to market and are languishing in the scientific literature or a psychologist's file cabinet.

A few of the tests in this book were developed by yours truly to fill a particular void. It was necessary for me to develop the test of cognitive ability in Part IV, for instance, because researchers have little interest in working on such an instrument when there are dozens of commercial tests of this type available. Because such tests are so widely used by employers, I thought it important to provide you with an example here. Your score on this test will provide a good indication of the score you could expect to receive on any number of copyrighted tests.

An important point to remember is that all of the tests in this book are of the self-report variety. This means that while they provide employers and career counselors with an efficient means of gathering information about you, they cannot generate any information that you are unwilling to provide. So, you will not learn anything potentially upsetting about yourself by taking these tests. You may not be happy with all of your scores, but the odds are good that you already have some understanding of your limitations. My hope is that by helping you to clearly articulate your limitations, you will find it easier to make the necessary changes for a satisfying and successful career.

I also hope that these tests will provide you with the specific information you will need to formulate a plan that will help you achieve success and career satisfaction. This means some hard work for you. You have to be prepared to think hard about the results of the tests and their implications. You have to be prepared to address your weaknesses—never an easy task. The tools you will need to do this are here. The rest is up to you.

To allow you to compare yourself with your competition, I have provided you with five reference points with which to evaluate the test results. These reference points are expressed in percentile scores, which tell you how you compare with the standardization sample and, by inference, the rest of society. So, if you have a percentile score of 15, that means that your score is higher than 15 percent of people who take the test. Similarly, a percentile score of 30 means that your score is higher than 30 percent of those who take the test, a percentile score of 70 is higher than 70 percent of those who take the test, and so on. The five reference points provided for each test are percentile scores of 15, 30, 50, 70, and 85. This will allow you to determine if your score is average, modestly above or below average, or substantially above or below average.

Okay. You are ready to begin. Be honest with yourself, be prepared to learn, and most important of all, enjoy the process of self-discovery.

Getting Started

After taking the tests in Part I, you will have a clearer picture of your vocational interests and you will know how mature your level of career planning is. These are the tests in Part I:

CHAPTER 1

The Reading Interest Inventory

The items below describe the subject matter of books and magazines. Your task is to determine how much interest you would have in reading such material. Use the following scale to indicate your level of interest in each subject.

7 = Extremely Interested
6 = Interested
5 = Somewhat Interested
4 = Neither Interested nor Disinterested
3 = Somewhat Disinterested
2 = Disinterested
1 = Extremely Disinterested

* Reprinted with permission of Louis H. Janda. The author wishes to thank Ryan P. Dickerson for his assistance in the development of this test.

_5_ 1. Art

_5_ 2. Painting

_5_ 3. Home Decoration

_4_ 4. Antiques

_24_ _5_ 5. Crafts

_4_ 6. Carpentry

_2_ 7. Construction

_4_ 8. Automobiles

_2_ 9. Engineering

_15_ _3_ 10. Architecture

_1_ 11. Chemistry

_3_ 12. Electronics

_3_ 13. Mathematics

_4_ 14. Computers

_13_ _2_ 15. Physical Science

_5_ 16. Scripture

_6_ 17. Religion

_6_ 18. Education

_4_ 19. Family/Child

_25_ _4_ 20. Literature

_4_ 21. Wildlife

_2_ 22. Hunting/Fishing

_2_ 23. Outdoor Recreation

_2_ 24. Marine Life

_15_ _5_ 25. Conservation

_3_ 26. Thriller

_1_ 27. Horror

_4_ 28. Mystery

_4_ 29. Science Fiction

_16_ _4_ 30. Fantasy

_3_ 31. Audio Equipment

_6_ 32. Music

_4_ 33. Comedy

_4_ 34. Film

_21_ _4_ 35. Humor

_4_ 36. Fitness/Exercise

_2_ 37. Sports

_5_ 38. Health

_5_ 39. Dieting

_22_ _6_ 40. Travel

_4_ 41. Geography

_4_ 42. History

_3_ 43. Maps

_4_ 44. Biography

_17_ _2_ 45. Westerns

_7_ 46. Psychology

_7_ 47. Philosophy

_6_ 48. Sociology

_2_ 49. Biology

_26_ _5_ 50. Occult

---

7 = Extremely Interested; 6 = Interested; 5 = Somewhat Interested;
4 = Neither Interested nor Disinterested; 3 = Somewhat Disinterested;
2 = Disinterested; 1 = Extremely Disinterested

SCORING

The fifty items on the scale are grouped into ten areas. Following are the areas and the corresponding items. Add your responses together to find your score in each area.

AREA	ITEMS
Arts and Crafts (RI1)	1 5
Mechanical (RI2)	6–10
Science/Math (RI3)	11–15
Religion/Scripture (RI4)	16–20
Wildlife/Outdoors (RI5)	21–25
Fiction (RI6)	26–30
Entertainment (RI7)	31–35
Fitness/Sports (RI8)	36–40
Geography/History (RI9)	41–45
Psychology/Philosophy (RI10)	46–50

NORMS

SCORES										PERCENTILE
RI1	RI2	RI3	RI4	RI5	RI6	RI7	RI8	RI9	RI10	
M F	M F	M F	M F	M F	M F	M F	M F	M F	M F	
25 26	28 18	26 23	26 30	30 29	31 29	31 31	30 33	22 25	28 30	85
22 24	25 16	23 20	23 27	27 26	28 26	29 28	28 30	19 22	26 27	70
19 21	22 13	20 17	20 23	24 22	24 23	27 25	25 26	16 18	23 23	50
16 18	19 10	17 14	17 19	21 18	20 20	25 22	22 22	13 14	20 19	30
13 16	16 8	14 11	14 16	18 15	17 17	23 19	20 19	10 11	18 16	15

High scores indicate greater interest. So, for example, if you received a percentile score of 70 on RI1, this means that 70 percent of people have less interest in Arts and Crafts than you do.

For more information see W. C. Tirre and S. Dixit, "Reading Interests: Their Dimensionality and Correlation with Personality and Cognitive Factors," *Personality and Individual Differences* 18 (1995): 731–38.

ABOUT THE READING INTERESTS TEST

Tests designed to measure vocational interests date back to the 1920s, when the Strong Vocational Interest Blank was first published. This test has gone through numerous revisions over the years, and more than a dozen additional tests have been added to career counselors' armamentarium, to aid them in their effort to find satisfying careers for their charges. Almost all of these tests are based on the rather curious premise that it is best to measure career interests indirectly. So, rather than asking questions such as Would you enjoy being a lawyer? these tests include questions such as Would you rather visit an art gallery or a natural history museum? The argument is that most people do not have enough information about the day-to-day activities of people in various careers to make an informed choice. So these tests are based on a strategy of finding common patterns of interests. If, for example, a majority of attorneys prefer museums over art galleries and you indicated a preference for museums, the assumption is that you would enjoy being an attorney.

While tests such as the Strong are clearly useful (about half of all test takers settle in the profession suggested by the test results), recent research suggests that people are fully capable of identifying their career interests in a straightforward manner. If you believe that you would be happy as a doctor, the odds are good that you would be. If you suspect you would hate being a store manager, you are justi-

fied in avoiding this career path. We are learning that career interests are not as mysterious as some test publishers would have us believe.

However, in the tradition of providing you with at least a somewhat indirect measure of your career interests, Old Dominion University psychology major Ryan Dickerman and I developed the Reading Interests Inventory. Inspired by the work of Drs. William Tirre and Sharvari Dixit of the Armstrong Laboratory at Brooks Air Force Base in Texas, we looked at the relationship between reading interests and vocational interests. Let me summarize what we found.

If you had a high score on Arts and Crafts, not surprisingly your first career choice probably involves occupations such as art teacher or commercial artist. Your second choice would be in the entertainment field, including occupations such as artist, actor, or musician. You probably would not enjoy occupations involving law enforcement such as police officer, security guard, or a military career.

A high score on the Mechanical cluster reflects an interest in occupations such as mechanical engineer, automobile mechanic, or machinist. Perhaps somewhat surprisingly, for a second choice you might consider the occupations of sales representative or stockbroker. You probably do not have a strong aversion to any occupations, but you are unlikely to have any interest in the service industry (e.g., travel agent, customer representative) or the helping professions (e.g., social worker, psychologist).

We were surprised to find that a high score on the third cluster, Science/Math, had the strongest relationship with a preference for the occupations of wildlife manager and park ranger. A close second, however, were the more predictable occupations of chemist, biologist, and research professor.

The results for the fourth cluster, Religion/Scripture, were also somewhat surprising. High scores indicated the strongest preference for the occupations of artist, actor, and musician. The helping professions, though, were a close second.

There were no surprises with the fifth cluster, Wildlife/Outdoors. High scorers indicated a strong preference for the occupations of wildlife manager, landscaper, and park ranger. While high scorers also expressed a fairly strong interest in the occupation of research scientist, it was a distant second.

Scores on the sixth cluster, Fiction, had modest relationships with many occupations but did not strongly correlate with any. Interestingly, the first choice of high scorers was the entertainment field, and the second choice was research scientist. It would seem that fiction devotees have eclectic tastes.

There was a mild surprise concerning high scorers on the seventh cluster, Entertainment. As anyone would predict, they showed a strong interest in the entertainment field, but they were equally interested in occupations such as office manager, accountant, stockbroker, and real estate sales. On the other hand, high scorers had a mild aversion to the occupation of research scientist.

Those whose reading interests focused on Fitness/Sports were also most attracted to the entertainment industry. Not far behind, however, were the occupations of wildlife manager and park ranger. A mild surprise was that these people had no interest in the law enforcement field. Perhaps I am the only one who holds such a stereotype, but I would have guessed that people who are interested in their fitness would have an interest in using their physical abilities to help keep society orderly.

High scores on the ninth cluster, Geography/History, were also related to a preference for the entertainment industry. Not far behind were the occupations of commercial artist, social worker, and physician. High scorers on this cluster were also an eclectic group; they showed some interest in almost all occupations.

The tenth cluster, Psychology/Philosophy, was perhaps the most predictable. High scorers showed a strong preference for the occupations of physician, psychologist, and social worker. Interestingly, people who enjoyed reading in this area showed relatively strong interests in most occupations. The only exceptions were the law enforcement and mechanical fields.

If you did not have high scores on any of the clusters, do not despair. Indeed, it may prove to be an advantage in the long run. It has been found that college students who have flat occupational interest profiles on tests such as the Strong are actually more satisfied with their careers ten years later than students who have clear occupational preferences. Students who do not know what they are interested in are more likely to experiment, to try out a variety of jobs. This process of trial and error does seem to be valuable in the quest to find a satisfying career. The moral of the story is clear: Do not be afraid to try various jobs, and do not be afraid to make a change if you are not happy with your initial choices.

CHAPTER 2
The Career Decisions Scale

Following is a list of statements about your career and education decisions. Read each statement. If you agree or mostly agree with the statement, mark a *T* in the space provided. If you disagree or mostly disagree with the statement, mark an *F* in the space provided.

---

* Reprinted with permission of Dr. Bert W. Westbrook.

F　1. I have decided how I can finance my education.

T　2. I have not yet decided when I would like to be living on my own.

F　3. I have not yet decided if I want to go with college or with a technical institute to further my career.

T　4. I have not yet decided where I am going to work.

F　5. I have no idea when I will get married.

F　6. I have not yet decided whether to become involved in the armed forces.

F　7. I have not decided when I will go to work full time.

T　8. I have not yet decided where I would like to go to work.

T　9. I have not yet decided what I want to major in.

F　10. I am not sure if I should work and go to school at the same time.

F　11. I have not yet decided whether to work full time or get further education.

T　12. I have not yet decided what specific job I would like to have.

T　13. I am not sure if I want to work mostly with people or things.

F　14. I have decided what I am going to do with my life, and my decision will be the same next year.

T　15. I have made practically no decision about my future.

F　16. I have made most of the necessary decisions about my future.

T　17. I haven't decided what my elective courses will be next year.

T　18. I would describe my career plans as "uncertain" at this time.

F　19. I would describe my career plans as "very uncertain" at this time.

F　20. I have made a decision about the general area that I want to work in for the rest of my life.

SCORING

Add your correct responses together to find your score.

1. T	11. F		
2. F	12. F		
3. F	13. F		
4. F	14. T		
5. F	15. F		
6. F	16. T		
7. F	17. F		
8. F	18. F		
9. F	19. F		
10. F	20. T		

NORMS

SCORE	PERCENTILE
15	85
13	70
11	50
9	30
7	15

A high score indicates a greater level of career decision making. If you, for instance, received a percentile score of 70, it means that 70 percent of young adults have not made as many career decisions as you have.

For more information see Bert W. Westbrook, E. Sanford, P. O'Neil, D. F. Horne, J. Fleenor, and R. Garren, "Predictive and Construct Validity of Six Experimental Measures of Career Maturity," *Journal of Vocational Behavior* 27 (1985): 338–55.

About the Career Decisions Scale

North Carolina State University psychologist Dr. Bert W. Westbrook has devoted the past twenty-five years of his career to developing the Career Planning Questionnaire. His test has evolved as changes occur in the understanding of how people come to make decisions about the occupations they wish to pursue. The test items have gone through numerous revisions, and the name of the test has changed over time as well. The first version, developed in 1970—the Cognitive Vocational Maturity Test—reflected the prevailing view of the 1970s that a mature approach to making career decisions reflected intellectual ability and was simply one aspect of a more general maturity. Westbrook believed, however, that it was possible to develop a relatively pure test of vocational maturity—that is, one that did not overlap with more general characteristics. To make a long story short, he published the latest version of his scale, the Career Planning Questionnaire, in 1987. It is intended to be used as a tool to provide a diagnosis of the rate and progress of the career development of young adults.

The Career Planning Questionnaire is comprised of six scales, five of which I have reproduced here. Since it requires a great deal of time to complete the entire test, I have chosen to present it as five distinct tests. This may have the added advantage of allowing you to more fully understand how you stand on the various elements of career maturity. The first

scale—the one you just completed—is the Career Decisions Scale. Let us take a closer look at it.

One of the frustrating aspects about being a psychology professor is that we seem to attract a number of students who are doing nothing more than marking time. We do have our share of serious, dedicated students who know they want a career in the field, but we also get those students who are majoring in psychology because they have nothing better to do. Last semester I advised a young woman, I'll call her Gale, who began our meeting by stating, "I have no idea what to take next semester." I handed her a list of the courses offered by our department and asked her which ones interested her the most. After studying the list for a minute or two she replied, "None of them look interesting." Naturally, I was curious as to why she was majoring in psychology, and when I asked her, Gail simply shrugged and said, "I don't know what else to major in." I am sympathetic to young adults who are anxious about making a decision that will so deeply affect their lives, but I cannot understand those people who seem to have no interest in even exploring the possibilities.

On the other hand, I have met a number of students over the years who took psychology courses to discover if they had any interest in the area. Janis represents this type of student. She was in the second semester of her sophomore year when she took my course in abnormal psychology, but she had yet to declare a major. After receiving a solid A on the midterm, Janis made an appointment to talk with me about careers in psychology. She admitted, somewhat nervously, that she had no idea what field she wanted to go into and wanted to learn more about what psychology had to offer. Apparently what I had to say was not impressive, since the last time I talked with her, she was taking several classes in the business department.

The point I want to make is that there are two types of people who are likely to receive low scores on the Career Decisions Scale. If your score was below the 50th percentile, you should try to determine in which category you belong. Gale represents the first category. These people are floundering. They are wasting their time and their money (or, in most cases, their parents' money). It is not important to have arrived at a clear career plan before finishing high school or entering college, but it is important to pursue one's education with the intent to learn about the possibilities. Because Gale had no interest in even trying to make career decisions, she had even less interest in her classes. She earned mostly C's but had enough D's and F's on her record to be suspended from the university after her sophomore year.

If you are reading this book, the odds are good that you fall into the category represented by Janis. There is certainly nothing wrong, or even unusual, about entering college without having made a career decision, as long as you are motivated to use your college coursework to do so in the future. I can understand Janis's frustration about not being able to settle on a major, and I greatly admire her

approach to resolving her uncertainty. She took her classes seriously and used her contacts with her professors as opportunities to learn more about each discipline. Perhaps Janis will not arrive at a clear decision by the time she graduates—I have known other students like her who did not. But a proactive approach to her dilemma will put her that much closer to making such decisions. And as long as she persists in actively collecting information and experiences, the odds are excellent she will find a career that is gratifying for her.

College is not the only solution for those of you who are actively trying to make career decisions. If you received a low score on the scale, you might find it more useful to try out jobs in construction, sales, the travel industry, or in any number of other fields. I've known many people who had a much clearer sense of what they wanted to do after a stint in the military or after spending six months backpacking through Europe. It does not especially matter what you do as long as you take an active approach to resolving your uncertainty.

The people who are likely to suffer in the long run are those who settle for the path of least resistance. These people take the first reasonable job they can get after graduating from high school or college, and before they know it, they have spent their entire working lives in a career that does not interest them. They spend their days counting the hours until they can go home and their weeks counting the days until their next vacation. It is never too late to make a career change, but it is much easier to do so when you are in your late teens or early twenties, rather than in your late forties or early fifties.

If you received a high score on the Career Decisions Scale, you are fortunate; you have a sense of direction that, at the very least, will motivate you to explore possibilities. But based on my experience, one cautionary note is warranted. I probably would have received a very high score on the Career Decisions Scale even before I was old enough to drive. I am not sure why, but by the time I was fourteen years old, I knew I wanted to be a clinical psychologist. I declared psychology as my major the day I entered college and entered a graduate program the fall after receiving my B.S. degree. There was no doubt in my mind about what I wanted to do with my life, until, that is, my third year of graduate school.

Clinical practicum was required in the third year of my graduate training. It was my first opportunity to use the knowl-edge I had gained in my years of course-work to help other people. Perhaps you can imagine my distress when I discovered that psychotherapy was not something I wanted to do on a full-time basis. I found it gratifying to help people resolve their problems, and I still do. But I also learned that I would be miserable if I had to do it for eight hours per day, five days per week. I simply found it to be too intense.

I was lucky because at about the same time I began work on my dissertation and discovered that I loved everything about the process of research. It turned out to be relatively easy for me to change my career direction. So, if you did receive a high score on the Career Decisions Scale, remain open to the possibility that you will have to make some adjustments in your plans as you get closer to your goal. As long as you remain flexible and open to a variety of possibilities, the odds are excellent that you will have a gratifying career.

CHAPTER 3

The Career Activities Scale

Below is a list of statements about different activities. Read each statement. If you have participated in that activity, mark the statement with a *T* in the space provided. If you have not done that activity, mark the space with an *F*.

---

* Reprinted with permission of Dr. Bert W. Westbrook.

_T_ 1. I have taken part in a job interview.

_T_ 2. I have taken a course that helped me to learn about the world of work.

_F_ 3. I have attended a "job fair" or "career day" where workers or employers talk about jobs.

_F_ 4. I have spent a lot of time thinking about the steps that are necessary for me to reach my career goals.

_T_ 5. I have spent a lot of time trying to figure out what I want in a job.

_T_ 6. I have done some reading and/or studying about the ways that people advance in the occupation I am considering.

_F_ 7. I have read something about the cost of getting trained for a career that I am interested in.

_F_ 8. I have looked into the educational requirements of an occupation that I am interested in.

_T_ 9. I have taken a close look at my past performance in school courses, extracurricular activities, and so forth, to understand what my abilities are.

_F_ 10. I have done several things that have helped me figure out my educational and career plans.

_F_ 11. I have talked to a career counselor about the connection between my interests and occupations.

_F_ 12. I have talked to a career counselor about the occupations that are appropriate for my abilities.

_F_ 13. I have taken a test to measure my vocational abilities.

_F_ 14. I have talked to friends or acquaintances to see if they think I have the abilities I think I have.

_F_ 15. I have observed workers in the occupation I may enter.

_T_ 16. I have read brochures about jobs in industries to obtain information about occupations.

_F_ 17. I have used the *Occupational Outlook Handbook* to get information about occupations.

_T_ 18. I have examined why I want to enter a particular occupation.

_F_ 19. I have figured out how I will pay for the cost of preparing for an occupation.

_F_ 20. I have read something about the abilities required in my preferred occupation.

SCORING

Add your correct responses together to find your score.

1. T	11. T
2. T	12. T
3. T	13. T
4. T	14. T
5. T	15. T
6. T	16. T
7. T	17. T
8. T	18. T
9. T	19. T
10. T	20. T

NORMS

SCORE	PERCENTILE
14	85
12	70
10	50
8	30
6	15

High scores mean that you have engaged in more career activities than other people in your situation. If, for example, you received a percentile score of 85, it means that 85 percent of people have engaged in fewer career activities than you have.

For more information see B. W. Westbrook, E. Sanford, P. O'Neil, D. F. Horne, J. Fleenor, and R. Garren, "Predictive and Construct Validity of Six Experimental Measures of Career Maturity," *Journal of Vocational Behavior* 27 (1985): 338–55.

ABOUT THE CAREER ACTIVITIES SCALE

The Career Activities Scale continues the theme that I introduced in the previous section, namely, that the best way to reach career decisions is to take an active, assertive approach to learning as much as you can about the possibilities. If you received a score above the 50th percentile on this test, keep on doing what you are doing. Your efforts will bear fruit. If you have not yet settled on a career you would like to pursue, the odds are good that you will, and relatively soon.

I have two words for those of you who scored below the 50th percentile: Get busy. It seems to me that many people who have no idea of what occupations they might find interesting expect that they will receive the answer in a sudden flash of insight. Perhaps that has happened to a few people, but it is much likelier that your answers will come as a result of your efforts. So there is no need to wander through the desert waiting for inspiration to strike. The items on this scale provide a number of ideas as to where you can begin. Attend all the job fairs and career day workshops you can, make an appointment to talk to the career counselor at your high school or college, and go to the library and read the *Occupational Outlook Handbook.* This book provides information about the approximately 250 occupations that account for six out of every seven jobs in our economy. It provides you with the educational and experience requirements for entering a specific occupation, and it provides forecasts

for jobs that will be in high demand in the future. It will even give you guidelines as to find a job and evaluate a job offer. Take advantage of every opportunity to learn as much as you can about as many different occupations as possible. Sooner or later you will hear something that will hit a responsive chord.

I think one mistake many high school students make is to assume that the school's career or vocational counselor is there only to help those students who do not plan to go on to college. This simply is not true. They are there to help everyone who needs a little help in finding the right direction. So, even if you are certain you want to continue your education, you should visit your counselor if you are not sure what field to pursue. Your counselor has devoted his or her career to helping people exactly like you and can be a rich source of information.

I believe the single most useful thing you can do to get the information you need is to talk to people who are in the occupations that strike you as possibilities. Your parents, friends of parents, school counselors, or college professors can all help to put you in touch with people in nearly any occupation. Once you have a name, do not hesitate to call to make an appointment to speak with this person. Yes, some people will say no to you, but a majority will be flattered to have the opportunity to share their experiences with you. These visits can add texture and depth to the information you find in books. The *Occupational Outlook Handbook* can provide you with a great deal of valuable information, but it will not give you a sense of the frustrations as well as the satisfactions that are part of every occupation.

The final suggestion I have, one that is not reflected by the items on this scale, is to read autobiographies or biographies about people in the fields that you believe might interest you. If you are interested in computers, for instance, you may learn more about the field by reading Bill Gates's *The Road Ahead*. People interested in biology will find James Watson's book, *The Double Helix: A Personal Account of the Discovery of the Structure of DNA*, both fascinating and instructive. Those of you who think you might like a career in architecture will learn something important from reading Brendan Gill's *Many Masks: A Life of Frank Lloyd Wright*. And as a final example, aspiring musicians should read *Rachmaninoff: Composer, Pianist, Conductor*. Books such as these can provide you with not only a sense of the day-to-day activities of people in the occupation but also a clearer idea of what it takes to succeed in the field. To illustrate, there have been times when I thought I should have gone into the financial field. I have always admired the mutual fund managers and investment advisors who appear on *Wall Street Week*, and I used to believe I would do quite well in such

occupations. I changed my mind, however, after reading Peter Lynch's *Beat the Street*. Lynch was the manager for Fidelity's Magellan Fund during the years when it experienced phenomenal growth. But after reading how he left for work at 6:00 A.M. every morning and spent up to eight hours of each of his rare vacation days on the telephone, I was not so sure I would want to change places with him. I knew I would not change places with him when I learned that he spent much of his working day pouring over the financial reports of hundreds of different companies. I have tried to read the annual reports of the few companies I do own a little stock in, and I can never make it to the last page. As intriguing as the world of investments appears from a distance, I learned the reality would be, for me, an anathema.

If, as in my case, the only purpose reading a book serves is to rule out a potential occupation, it will be well worth your time. Remember, as long as you continue to take an active approach to learning about occupations that might be right for you, you will eventually find one that fits with your interests and abilities. And the more active you are in your search for information, the sooner this will happen.

CHAPTER 4
The Career
Salience Scale

The following statements are about the importance of a career to you. If you agree with the statement, mark a *T* in the space provided. If you disagree with the statement, mark an *F*.

* Reprinted with permission of Dr. Bert W. Westbrook.

F 1. Being successful in my line of work is more important than finding the right person to marry.

____ 2. Being successful in my line of work is more important than having lots of money.

____ 3. Having strong friendships is more important than being successful in my line of work.

____ 4. Being successful in my line of work is less important than having a good social life.

T 5. Spending time with parents and friends is more important than spending time on my job.

____ 6. Being a leader in my community is more important than being successful in my line of work.

____ 7. Working to correct social and economic inequalities is just as important as working to get ahead in my career.

____ 8. Having leisure time to enjoy my own interests is more important than getting ahead in my career.

T 9. Spending time in community and service organizations is just as important as spending time in my line of work.

T 10. Spending time with a hobby is just as important as spending time in my full-time job.

F 11. I would not keep a job that ever requires me to go to school in my spare time.

T 12. I would not take a job that requires me to move around the country.

T 13. Having time to read, think, and discuss important questions about life is just as important as getting ahead in my career.

T 14. I would not take a job that does not permit me to do what I think is right.

F 15. I would rather have a job that will give me a lot of leisure time away from work than a job that will allow me to make my own decisions.

___T___ 16. There are things that I enjoy more than work.

___F___ 17. I would rather spend my time in recreational activities than in my career.

___F___ 18. I will make many sacrifices to get ahead in my career.

___F___ 19. A job with high income is more important to me than a job that will allow me to help others.

___F___ 20. I would move to another part of the country if that is what it takes for me to succeed in my career.

SCORING

Add your correct responses together to find your score.

1. T	11. F
2. T	12. F
3. F	13. F
4. F	14. F
5. F	15. F
6. F	16. F
7. F	17. F
8. F	18. T
9. F	19. T
10. F	20. T

NORMS

SCORE	PERCENTILE
14	85
13	70
11	50
9	30
8	15

High scores indicate that a successful career is important to you. If, for instance, you received a percentile score of 50, it means that 50 percent of people place less importance on having a successful career than you do.

For more information see B. W. Westbrook, E. Sanford, P. O'Neil, D. F. Horne, J. Fleenor, and R. Garren, "Predictive and Construct Validity of Six Experimental Measures of Career Maturity," *Journal of Vocational Behavior* 27 (1985): 338–55.

ABOUT THE CAREER SALIENCE SCORE

If you are reading this book, the odds are good that you received a score above the 50th percentile on the Career Salience Scale. As you can tell from the content of the items, a high score on this scale indicates a desire to be successful and a willingness to make sacrifices to achieve that success. You would not be reading this book if these were issues that did not concern you.

If, by chance, you received a score below the 50th percentile on this scale, I would simply say, "Good for you." I feel fortunate to have had a challenging career that has provided me with the opportunity to experience a few successes, minor as they may be. I am not sure I would have enjoyed my life as much as I have had I not had a job that allowed me the numerous chances to become excited about my next project. From my perspective, I believe that a gratifying career is central to a satisfying life. But, on the other hand, I have known a number of people who perceived work quite differently from me and had highly satisfying lives nonetheless.

Joe and Sharon, for instance, decided that an abundance of leisure time is what they want from life. Joe has a small carpet business that he operates out of the back of his van. He helps customers with their selections and then passes the order on to his team of installers. Ten hours of work is a busy week for Joe. Sharon teaches junior high school. While she enjoys her job, she has never had thoughts about "getting ahead," and she plans to retire as soon as she has her thirty years in. Together they make a comfortable living, and their schedule makes it possible for them to play golf together every day during the summer. Sharon puts her clubs away as soon as the weather turns cold, but Joe manages to get in three or four rounds per week throughout the year, with enough time left over to see every new movie within a few days of its release. Joe and Sharon will be retiring within a year, but it is difficult for me to see how their lives will be much different.

At times, a small part of me has envied Joe and Sharon. During those occasional weeks when I was working twelve hours per day to meet a deadline, I wondered why I did not have enough sense to arrange my life the way Joe has. But I know that without my projects, even with their onerous deadlines, I would feel somewhat empty and directionless. But I do not believe that my view of life and work are necessarily superior to the views of Joe and Sharon. We have each found an approach that works best for us.

One concern I had with a number of the items on the Career Salience Scale is that they implied that one has to make a choice between two goals that are not necessarily mutually exclusive. With respect to item 1, for instance, I believe I did find the right person to marry *and* have achieved a modicum of success in my career. As a second example, career success and money do not always go hand in hand, as item 2 suggests, but they tend to be highly correlated. It is realistic to strive for both success and a healthy income. And contrary to what item 3 suggests, there is no need to choose between having strong friendships and being successful in one's work. Indeed, to me the two seem to go together. Most of the people I consider friends are people I have met through work. And while there are many times when we cannot get together for a round of golf or dinner because of our work schedules, we do manage to find plenty of time to socialize despite our commitment to our careers. As a final example, item 6 suggests that being a leader in one's community and being successful in one's career are mutually exclusive. Again, it seems to me that many people (although I am not one of them) manage to do both. In Virginia Beach, my hometown, virtually everyone on the city council is extremely successful in his or her career. One of the most successful attorneys in my community is perhaps best known for his volunteer work for a major charitable organization. Successful people tend to be energetic and have a zest for life that allows them to engage in a variety of activities. Often, it is the not-so-successful people who complain that they do not have time for hobbies or community work. But these are the same people who can provide you with a synopsis of twenty to thirty television shows.

One last thought about Career Salience: Be prepared for your score on this scale to change at different points in your life. I know my score would have been much lower when I was twenty than when I was in my thirties. Now that I am in my early fifties, it is probably somewhat lower than it was ten years ago. When I was twenty, I had yet to have a job that I could tolerate, much less enjoy. I viewed work as a necessary evil that one had to endure in order to eat. Indeed, my primary motive for going to graduate school was to put off entering the work force for a few more years. But halfway into my first year as a college professor, I was hooked. I was surprised by how much I enjoyed teaching and how important it was to me to be good at it. I was also surprised that I could lose myself for hours on end while working on a research project. For ten to fifteen years I looked forward to the end of vacations so that I could get back to work. Perhaps I am slowing down, but currently I find myself less willing to forgo leisure time because of my work demands. I still have to have an interesting project going to keep my spirits up, but I no longer feel capable of working through the evening as I once did so easily.

It seems to me that finding the right balance is most important, and this balance is different for different people. My balance now is different than it was fifteen years ago, and it has always been different than Joe's and Sharon's. What is really important is to find several aspects of life that you can find compelling. Of those who received a low score on this scale, the only ones who should be concerned are those who cannot find anything in life that gets their blood flowing.

CHAPTER 5

The Career Concerns Scale

The following statements are about concerns that people have about their careers. Read each statement. If you agree with the statement, mark *T*. If you disagree with the statement, mark *F*.

---

* Reprinted with permission of Dr. Bert W. Westbrook.

___ 1. I have too many interests at this point to choose just one job.

___ 2. I don't know what you have to do to get into a job.

___ 3. There are so many job choices that I am confused.

___ 4. I can't fit my interests and values into one specific job.

___ 5. I am not sure that I'd be successful in today's world.

___ 6. I'm not sure I want to spend so many years in school after high school.

___ 7. I don't know what courses to take to get into my preferred job.

___ 8. I am not sure that I can afford to get the education required in my career.

___ 9. I don't know much about the requirements for getting the job I have thought about.

___ 10. I am concerned whether there will be a need for my career in the future.

___ 11. I need to know more requirements about the job I have thought about.

___ 12. I am not sure whether I can get qualified for the careers I am interested in.

___ 13. I am not sure whether I will like my job once I get started.

___ 14. My problem is that after studying for my job choice, I don't know what to do next.

___ 15. I am not sure whether I am headed in the right direction.

___ 16. I just don't know what to do about my future career.

___ 17. I don't know what I am capable of doing.

___ 18. I don't really know what courses to take in school.

___ 19. I don't know what I'd be good at.

___ 20. I don't have enough information about how much money can be earned in the job I like.

SCORING

Add your correct responses together to find your score.

1.	T	11.	T
2.	T	12.	T
3.	T	13.	T
4.	T	14.	T
5.	T	15.	T
6.	T	16.	T
7.	T	17.	T
8.	T	18.	T
9.	T	19.	T
10.	T	20.	T

NORMS

SCORE	PERCENTILE
17	85
15	70
12	50
9	30
7	15

High scores indicate a greater level of career concerns. If, for instance, you received a percentile score of 70, it means that 70 percent of young adults have fewer career concerns than you do.

For more information see B. W. Westbrook, E. Sanford, P. O'Neil, D. F. Horne, J. Fleenor, and R. Garren, "Predictive and Construct Validity of Six Experimental Measures of Career Maturity," *Journal of Vocational Behavior* 27 (1985): 338–55.

ABOUT THE CAREER CONCERNS SCALE

One of my jobs as a college professor is advising college students. When my advisees reach their junior year, one question I always ask is, What are you going to do after you graduate? Many of my students have clear plans; they intend to go on to graduate school or medical or law school. Others have had a specific job in mind for several years. This past year I had one psychology major who applied to be an FBI agent, another who intended to become an air traffic controller, and a third who was accepted as a management trainee at a large manufacturing company. Two other students have been developing plans to start their own businesses for years. Part-time jobs have provided them with relevant experience, they have investigated their potential competition extensively, and one has even found a partner to provide financing. I have confidence that these students will achieve the success they deserve.

Many other students, on the other hand, have no idea what they plan to do after graduation. "Maybe I'll go to graduate school" or "I suppose I'll look for a job" are responses I hear every semester. Other students, whose grades suggest they are quite capable, have almost no idea as to how to accomplish their goals. Perhaps it reflects a failure on my part, but I have students who are graduating with a degree in psychology who do not fully understand the difference between clinical psychology and psychiatry. More than once a student

has announced that he or she plans to be a psychiatrist only to be shocked to learn that graduation from medical school is a prerequisite. Other students have told me that they would like to go to graduate school but cannot afford to. These young men and women are pleasantly surprised when I tell them that most doctoral programs and many masters programs provide a paid research or teaching assistantship and a tuition waiver.

The point is that career concerns do not resolve themselves. One must take an active role to acquire the information necessary to determine the answers to the issues raised by the items on the Career Concerns Scale. If you received a low score on this test, you can remove much of your uncertainty if you resolve to spend an hour each week seeking relevant information. Let us talk about a few of the specific items.

Many of your questions can be answered quickly and easily if you spend a few hours browsing through the *Occupational Outlook Handbook*, perhaps the single most important source of information about various careers. You do not even have to make a visit to the library to take advantage of this invaluable resource. If you have Internet access, you can find the most recent edition of the handbook at http://stats.bls.gov/ocohome.htm. An advantage of the online version of the handbook is that it makes in painless to perform searches on the occupations that interest you the most.

The Internet, by the way, provides an abundance of information relevant to career concerns. As just one example, the American Psychological Association Web site includes a section specifically for students ranging from high school to graduate school. After browsing through this information for twenty minutes, aspiring psychologists will have a good idea about the courses they should take, student loans, accredited graduate programs, and potential careers in psychology. The site also provides an extensive list of additional resources for the curious student. Most professional organizations make similar information available via the Internet.

If you received a low score because it was difficult for you to narrow your interests, you are one of the fortunate ones. The people who are nearly impossible to help are those who are not interested in much of anything. If you are interested in several fields, continue to learn as much as you can about all of them by reading, browsing through relevant Web sites, and taking courses. It is usually the case that with more information, you will be able to decide which possibility holds the most appeal for you. Keep in mind that you are not wasting your time if you should change majors once or twice, or

work in quite different jobs over a period of a few years. You have a lifetime to develop your career, and these early experiences may serve you well in the long run. I have known several people who had extremely productive careers in psychology despite beginning their graduate work in their thirties and, in a few cases, in their forties. Indeed, their broad early experiences often served to make them better psychologists.

Finally, do not dismiss the possibility that you may be able to combine your interests in such a way as to make you especially appealing to a potential employer. I am obviously most familiar with psychology, and I could provide you with many examples of students who received attractive job offers because they integrated their interest in psychology with fields such as art, computer programming, marketing, and English. There are certain to be countless valuable combinations in a variety of fields. Indeed, some of the most innovative people are those whose knowledge bridges the gap between two disciplines. Your varied interests could well turn out to be to your advantage over the long run.

CHAPTER 6

The Career Values Scale

In each of the following statements, two jobs are described. Read the descriptions for the two jobs and decide which job you prefer. If you are not exactly sure which job you would choose, mark C.

---

* Reprinted with permission of Dr. Bert W. Westbrook.

_A_ 1. (A) In Job A people respect you, look up to you, and listen to your opinion; BUT you would not have the freedom to make your own decisions.

   (B) Job B would allow you to work in your one main field of interest, but you would be doing the same thing over and over.

   (C) I am not exactly sure.

_A_ 2. (A) Job A involves many different kinds of activities and problems, many changes, and new people to meet; but you would not be working in your one main field of interest.

   (B) Job B would allow you to work in your one main field of interest, but you would be doing the same thing over and over.

   (C) I am not exactly sure.

_A_ 3. (A) In Job A you would be able to make your own decisions, but helping others would not be a main part of your job.

   (B) In Job B helping others would be the main part of your job, but you would not be able to make your own decisions.

   (C) I am not exactly sure.

_X_ 4. (A) In Job A people respect you, look up to you, and listen to your opinion; but you may not be able to keep your job.

   (B) In Job B you would not be afraid of losing your job, but people would not look up to you and listen to your opinion.

   (C) I am not exactly sure.

_X_ 5. (A) Job A will allow you to make your own decisions, but it does not provide you with much security. You would be concerned with losing your job.

   (B) Job B is a very secure job, but you would not be able to make your own decisions.

   (C) I am not exactly sure which job I would chose.

_B_ 6. (A) In Job A helping others would be a main part of your job; but you would have long working hours and short vacations, and you would not be able to choose your own time off.

   (B) In Job B you would have short work hours, long vacations, and a chance to choose you own time off; but helping others would not be a main part of your job.

   (C) I am not exactly sure.

___ 7. (A) Job A will provide you with security, but your work will not be in your one main field of interest.

(B) Job B will be in your main field of interest, but it will not provide you with much security. You cannot count on keeping the job year after year.

(C) I am not exactly sure which job I would choose.

___ 8. (A) Job A will allow you to make your own decisions, but you would not be able to work in your main field of interest.

(B) Job B will allow you to work in your main field of interest, but you will not be allowed to make your own decisions.

(C) I am not exactly sure.

___ 9. (A) In Job A helping others would be a main part of your job; but you would not lead others, tell them what to do, or be responsible for their work.

(B) In Job B you would lead others, tell them what to do, and be responsible for their work; but helping others would not be a main part of your work.

(C) I am not exactly sure.

___ 10. (A) In Job A you would have the freedom to make your own decisions; but you would have long work hours, short vacations, and no chance to choose your own time off.

(B) In Job B you would have short work hours, long vacations, and the chance to choose your own time off; but you would not have the chance to make your own decisions.

(C) I am not exactly sure.

___ 11. (A) In Job A you would be able to make your own decisions, but you would not lead others, tell them what to do, or be responsible for their work.

(B) In Job B you would lead others, tell them what to do, and be responsible for their work; but you would not have the freedom to make your own decisions.

(C) I am not exactly sure.

B 12. (A) Job A will provide you with security, but your work will be monotonous; you will be doing the same thing over and over.

     (B) Job B would provide you with variety—different kinds of activities and problems, many, many changes, and new people to meet—but it will not provide you with security; you cannot count on keeping your job year after year.

     (C) I am not exactly sure.

A 13. (A) In Job A you would be able to make your own decisions, but you would be doing the same thing over and over.

     (B) In Job B you would be doing many different kinds of activities—new problems, places, and people—but you would not be able to make your own decisions.

     (C) I am not exactly sure.

A 14. (A) Job A will pay you more than enough to live on, but helping others will not be a main part of your job.

     (B) In Job B helping others would be the main part of your job, but your income would not allow you to have a lot of extra money.

     (C) I am not exactly sure.

B 15. (A) In Job A you would be leading others, telling them what to do, and taking responsibility for their work; but you would not have much time to spend away from your work.

     (B) In Job B you would be able to spend lots of time away from your work, but you would not be able to lead others.

     (C) I am not exactly sure.

B 16. (A) In Job A you would not be afraid of losing your job, but you would have to get many years of education before you could start working.

     (B) In Job B you could start working right away, but you could not count on keeping your job year after year.

     (C) I am not exactly sure.

B 17. (A) Job A will provide you with security, but you would not have much leisure time.

(B) Job B would provide you with lots of leisure time but not much job security.

(C) I am not exactly sure.

C 18. (A) Job A will provide you with a high income; but you will have to spend lots of time, effort, and money for more education.

(B) Job B will allow you to start working right after high school, with very little education or training, but you will not have a high income.

(C) I am not exactly sure.

A 19. (A) In Job A people would respect you, look up to you, and listen to your opinion; but you would not have a chance to lead others, tell them what to do, or be responsible for their work.

(B) In Job B you would be able to lead others, tell them what to do, and be responsible for their work; but people would not look up to you, listen to your opinion, or ask for your help.

(C) I am not exactly sure.

B 20. (A) In Job A people would respect you, look up to you, and listen to your opinion; but helping others would not be a main part of your job.

(B) In Job B helping others would be a main part of your job, but people would not look up to you or listen to your opinions.

(C) I am not exactly sure.

SCORING

The Career Values Scale is scored for ten values. The scoring procedure for this test is more complicated than for others in this book. Every A and B alternative counts plus 1 point on one scale and minus 1 point on another scale. To obtain your score on each scale, determine if you endorsed the alternative listed and either add or subtract one point as indicated.

PRESTIGE	INDEPENDENCE	HELPING OTHERS	SECURITY
1A +1	1A -1	3A -1	4A -1
4A +1	3A +1	3B +1	4B +1
4B -1	3B -1	6A +1	5A -1
19A +1	5A +1	6B -1	5B +1
19B -1	5B -1	9A +1	7A +1
20A +1	8A +1	9B -1	7B -1
20B -1	8B -1	14A -1	12A +1
	10A +1	14B +1	12B -1
2	10B -1	20A -1	16A +1
	11A +1	20B +1	16B -1
	11B -1		17A +1
	13A +1	-3	17B -1
	13B -1		
	5		-2

VARIETY	LEADERSHIP	FIELD OF INTEREST	LEISURE
1B -1	9A -1	1B +1	6A -1
2A +1	9B +1	2A -1	6B +1
2B -1	11A -1	2B +1	10A -1
7A -1	11B +1	7B +1	10B +1
12A -1	15A +1	8A -1	15A -1
12B +1	15B -1	8B +1	15B +1
13A -1	19A -1	-2	17A -1
13B +1	19B +1		17B +1
0	-2		0

EARLY ENTRY	INCOME
16A -1	14A +1
16B +1	14B -1
18A -1	18A +1
18B +1	18B -1
1	1

18 = C

NORMS*

(handwritten above columns: 60% 85% 30 20% 60% 35% 15% 50% 70% 70)

PR	IN	HO	SE	VA	LD	FI	LE	EE	IN	PERCENTILE
4	(5)	5	6	3	4	4	4	2	2	85
3	2	3	3	1	2	3	2	(1)	(1)	70
1	-1	0	0	-1	0	1	(0)	0	0	50
-1	-4	(-3)	-3	-3	(-2)	-1	-2	-1	-1	30
-2	-7	-5	-6	-5	-4	(-2)	-4	-2	-2	15

High scores indicate a greater importance for the value involved. If, for instance, you received a percentile score of 85 on Pr, it means that 85 percent of people place less importance on prestige than you do.

*These are not norms in the true sense of the term. Dr. Westbrook's norms reflected the number of items for which examinees selected either alternative A or B. The average for his normative sample was 14. This score reflected the degree to which examinees had developed career values. Low scores indicated a person who had not decided what values were important. I developed these "normative" scores to enable you to learn something about the relative strength of your career values.

For more information see B. W. Westbrook, E. Sanford, P. O'Neil, D. F. Horne, J. Fleenor, and R. Garren, "Predictive and Construct Validity of Six Experimental Measures of Career Maturity," *Journal of Vocational Behavior* 27 (1985): 338–55.

(handwritten notes:)

It appears to me that.

Independence is more important to me than security.

70% of us care about helping other people

40% of us want more variety.

85% of us feel Field of Interest is important

30% of us feel income is important or early city.

ABOUT THE CAREER VALUES SCALE

The importance of understanding one's values in selecting a satisfying career has been understood for more than half a century now. One well-known test that is now in its third edition, the Allport-Vernon-Lindzey Study of Values, was introduced in the 1930s to help young adults select an appropriate career path. A number of similar tests have been published over the years to serve as tools for vocational counselors to provide direction for their clients. But if you were to take one of these tests, you would pay considerably more than you did for this entire book. Dr. Westbrook's Career Values Scale will provide you with an excellent idea of the values that are especially important to you. If you are to have a satisfying career, you would be well advised to carefully consider the knowledge you gain from the results of this test.

Most jobs have both their strengths and weaknesses. My job as a college professor, for instance, provides me with a great deal of independence and variety. The university expects me to pursue my intellectual interests, and they do not especially care what those interests are as long as they result in some scholarly or educational product. Also, I have tenure (which provides excellent job security), and my job gives me the opportunity to help others. On the other hand, I did have to spend twenty years of my life in school before I could enter my profession, and I will never earn as much money as my colleagues working in private practice or business. Yes, given my preferences I would rather have it all, but the reality is that I cannot think of another job that provides a better fit with my values. Most jobs require similar trade-offs. I have several former students who went into sales, for example, and within a year their income was three times as much as mine. They had more than enough money to thoroughly enjoy their liberal vacation time; on the other hand, they knew that their jobs would last only as long as they continued to meet their quotas.

After you have determined the values that are most important to you, you can begin to explore whether the occupations you are considering will provide a good fit. Again, the best way to do this is by talking to people who are in those occupations. It is important that you talk to more than one person to ensure that you are getting a reasonable evaluation of the field. I have recently talked to two computer scientists, for instance, who had quite different things to say about their occupation. They both agreed that they had clear opportunities to earn a generous income, but beyond that their views had little in common. Mike, who worked in the computer center of a large university complained that he had virtually no opportunities to pursue his special interests and that after fifteen years of responding to the faculty's concerns, his job had become stultifying. Ken, on the other hand, worked for a small software development company, and he loved the variety that his job afforded and his ability to work independently. Mike, of course, had more job security than Ken, but this was not an important issue for either of them.

The important point is that different jobs in the same field might offer quite different opportunities to satisfy certain values. If a particular value is extremely important to you, you should not become discouraged if one person in that occupation tells you that you will not be able to satisfy your needs. The chances are good that you will be able find a job within most any occupation that will be a good match for your values.

This will pose more of a challenge in some fields than others. If helping others, for instance, is your primary value, it may be somewhat difficult to find a job that is right for you if your second most important value is a high income, since the helping professions are generally known for their modest pay scales. People with these values would want to select an occupation carefully. Psychiatrists, for instance, typically earn considerably more than social workers, although both occupations afford ample opportunities to help others. Similarly, physicians have higher incomes than nurses, although the explicit purpose of both occupations is to help others.

Dr. Westbrook's Career Values Scale is similar to most tests of this type in that it forces test takers to make choices between two values. (The technical term to describe this type of test is *ipsative*. All of the other tests in this book can be characterized as *normative* tests.) On item 1, for instance, people who select alternative A are indicating that prestige is more important to them than independence. This approach to test development is useful because it allows people to determine the order of importance in which they regard their values. It does, however, have an important limitation; namely, it does not distinguish between people who attach a similar level of importance to a variety of values and people who would rate the various values quite differently in terms of their importance. To illustrate, both the person who believes that prestige is only slightly more important than independence and the person who believes that independence is completely unimportant would select alternative A for item 1. Their scores, however, would not reflect the different weights they assign to the two values.

This approach to test development will produce results that can be misleading for some test takers. Perhaps you believe that all ten values measured by this test are at least somewhat important to you. But the way in which the test is structured will cause some of your scores to fall below the 50th percentile. So keep in mind that your test results only provide you with information about the order of importance that you attach to the various values. A high score for a particular value simply means that that value is more important to you than are the other values. Conversely, a low score does not necessarily mean that the value is unimportant to you; it only means that it is less important to you than are others.

PART II

Evaluating Where You Are Now

After taking the tests in this section, you will know how you compare with others in terms of how well you like your job, how committed you are to it, how stressful you find it, and how well you cope with stress. These are the tests in Part II:

CHAPTER 7

Hoppock's Job Satisfaction Questions

* Originally published in Robert Hoppock's *Job Satisfaction* (New York: Harper & Row, 1935).

Of the following statements, choose the ONE that best tells how well you like your job. Place a check mark in front of that statement.

1. ✓ I hate it.

2. ____ I dislike it.

3. ____ I don't like it.

4. ____ I am indifferent to it.

5. ____ I like it.

6. ____ I am enthusiastic about it.

7. ____ I love it.

Of the following statements, check the one that shows HOW MUCH OF THE TIME you feel satisfied with your job.

7. ____ All of the Time

6. ____ Most of the Time

5. ____ A Good Deal of the Time

4. ____ About Half of the Time

3. ____ Occasionally

2. ✓ Seldom

1. ____ Never

Of the following statements, check the ONE that best tells how you feel about changing your job.

1.____ I would quit this job at once if I could get anything else to do.

2.____ I would take almost any other job in which I could earn as much as I am earning now.

3._✓_ I would like to change both my job and my occupation.

4.____ I would like to exchange my present job for another job in the same line of work.

5.____ I am not eager to change my job, but I would do so if I could get a better job.

6.____ I cannot think of any jobs for which I would exchange mine.

7.____ I would not exchange my job for any other.

Of the following statements, check the one that shows how you think you compare with other people.

7.____ No one likes his or her job better than I like mine.

6.____ I like my job much better than most people like theirs.

5.____ I like my job better than most people like theirs.

4.____ I like my job about as well as most people like theirs.

3._✓_ I dislike my job more than most people dislike theirs.

2.____ I dislike my job much more than most people dislike theirs

1.____ No one dislikes his or her job more than I dislike mine.

SCORING

Add together the numbers that correspond to your responses.

NORMS

SCORE	PERCENTILE
23	85
21	70
18	50
15	30
13	15

High scores indicate greater job satisfaction. If, for instance, you received a percentile score of 85, it means that 85 percent of people are less satisfied with their jobs than you are.

For more information see C. W. McNichols, M. J. Stahl, and T. R. Manley, "A Validation of Hoppock's Job Satisfaction Measure," *Academy of Management Journal* 21 (1978): 737–42.

ABOUT HOPPOCK'S JOB SATISFACTION QUESTIONS

Psychological tests are not like wine: Rather than improving with age, they generally become obsolete with the passage of time. One of the very few exceptions is the brief test you just completed, known as Hoppock's Job Satisfaction Questions, published in 1935. Although there have been numerous attempts to create more sophisticated measures of job satisfaction over the years, Hoppock's instrument continues to be one of the most widely used of such measures. It offers the advantage of being extremely brief, yet the evidence strongly suggests it also provides an accurate measure of how satisfied people are with their jobs.

Because it has been used for so many years, the information about normative performance is extensive. The norms presented here are based on responses collected over the past decade of nearly thirty thousand people. The specific results depend on the type of workers being assessed. Generally, the higher people are on the ladder of occupational status, the greater their job satisfaction will be. Professional workers, for example, have an average job satisfaction score that is six to seven points higher than the average for clerical workers. It is interesting to note, however, that for most samples, ranging from the unskilled to the professional, there are always a few workers who receive the lowest possible score and a few others who receive the highest possible score. So, while there is a relationship between the type of

job one has and the likelihood that one will enjoy it, it is also true that any job can be either loved or hated by at least a few people. The key, of course, is to find a job that is right for you, the job that you can enjoy and derive satisfaction from regardless of how others view it. If your score was below the 50th percentile, it could suggest that you are in the wrong field. Be honest with yourself, though. If you have never had a job for which your score would be above the 50th percentile, perhaps the problem lies with your feelings about work in general and not your job.

Over the years a number of research studies have explored factors that might be related to job satisfaction. In one such study, Dr. McNichols and his colleagues, from the Air Force Institute of Technology, found that the salient factor was satisfaction with the work. That is, if employees enjoy their work, they are highly likely to be satisfied with their jobs. The second most important factor, which comes as no surprise, was satisfaction with one's supervisor. A good boss can make even the worst work tolerable, and a bad boss can make an otherwise ideal job unbearable. The third factor was perceived opportunity for promotions. If employees believe that management will provide opportunities for advancement, they are more likely to be satisfied with their jobs. A close fourth was satisfaction with coworkers. Everyone who has any work history knows that congenial colleagues can often make or break a job.

It might surprise you to learn that Dr. McNichols reported that pay had an extremely slight relationship with job satisfaction. This is a common finding. Most people, when asked what they like about their jobs, list factors such as interesting work and congenial colleagues—in other words, the first four factors identified by McNichols. But the reality is that if their pay was cut in half, their work could never be interesting enough to keep them on the job. Money is an extremely powerful motivator, and if people believe they are underpaid or if they believe they could earn more elsewhere, they are highly likely to be quite dissatisfied with their jobs. We are not always good at identifying what is most important to us.

If you did receive a low score on Hoppock's scale, you should develop a plan for changing your situation. Having a satisfying job is crucial to having a satisfying life. When asked about the secret of happiness, Sigmund Freud replied, "To love and to work." Over the course of a lifetime, the only activity we will spend more time engaged in than working is sleeping. So if you hate your job, you will need extraordinary luck in love if you are to find your life satisfying.

Keep in mind that it is never too late to make a change. Every semester I have several students in their forties and fifties who have returned to school because they want a more satisfying job. Yes, most of these people have to make extreme sacrifices in order to accomplish their goals, but when the alternative is hating every weekday, selling one's house and moving into an apartment for a couple of years seems like a small price to pay.

Most everyone has had a job they have hated. I still have painfully vivid memories of the summer I spent folding lake-liners—a huge piece of vinyl that was used to line the bottom of artificial lakes. But if you have to drag yourself to work for more than a year or two, you have no one to blame but yourself. There are a whole lot of alternatives out there. It is up to you to find them.

CHAPTER 8

The Work Commitment Index

The following statements reflect attitudes and perceptions that people can have about work in general and their job or career in particular. Use the scale below to indicate how accurately each statement describes your feelings or beliefs.

6 = Strongly Agree
5 = Agree
4 = Somewhat Agree
3 = Somewhat Disagree
2 = Disagree
1 = Strongly Disagree

---

* Reprinted with permission of Dr. Gary Blau.

2

5

5

1

_5_ 1. If I could, I would go into a different occupation.

_2_ 2. I can see myself in my current occupation for many years to come.

_2_ 3. My choice of an occupation has proven to be a good decision.

_6_ 4. If I had it to do over again, I would not choose the same occupation.

6 *

6

6

4

_1_ 5. If I had enough money to be financially independent, I would still continue in my present occupation.

_1_ 6. Sometimes, I feel dissatisfied with my occupation.

_+_ 7. I like my occupation too much to ever give it up.

_3_ 8. My education and training was not relevant to my present occupation.

4

4

46   3

4

_3_ 9. I have selected the ideal occupation for my life's work.

_3_ 10. I wish I had chosen a different occupation.

_4_ 11. I am disappointed that I entered my present occupation.

_3_ 12. The most important things about my life involve my job.

2

4

3

4

5

27   5

_5_ 13. My job is only a small part of who I am.

_3_ 14. I live, eat, and breathe my job.

_4_ 15. Most of my interests center around my job.

_3_ 16. Most of my personal life goals are job oriented.

_2_ 17. My job is very central to my existence.

_2_ 18. I like to be absorbed in my job most of the time.

0

6

6

4

_1_ 19. Hard work makes one a better person.

_1_ 20. Wasting time is as bad as wasting money.

_1_ 21. People's worth is determined by how well they do their work.

_3_ 22. It is better to have work that demands much responsibility.

---

6 = Strongly Agree; 5 = Agree; 4 = Somewhat Agree;
3 = Somewhat Disagree; 2 = Disagree; 1 = Strongly Disagree

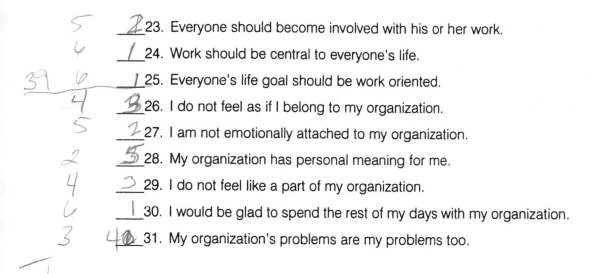

5   _2_ 23. Everyone should become involved with his or her work.

6   _1_ 24. Work should be central to everyone's life.

39 6 _1_ 25. Everyone's life goal should be work oriented.

4   _3_ 26. I do not feel as if I belong to my organization.

5   _2_ 27. I am not emotionally attached to my organization.

2   _3_ 28. My organization has personal meaning for me.

4   _3_ 29. I do not feel like a part of my organization.

6   _1_ 30. I would be glad to spend the rest of my days with my organization.

3   4_2_ 31. My organization's problems are my problems too.

24

SCORING

Before scoring this test, the following items must be reversed (i.e., 6 = 1, 5 = 2, 4 = 3, 3 = 4, 2 = 5, and 1 = 6): 4, 6, 8, 10, 11, 13, 26, 27, 29. The Work Commitment Index is comprised of four scales. Items 1 through 11 comprise the Occupational Commitment Scale (OcC), items 12 through 18 comprise the Job Involvement Scale (JI), items 19 through 25 comprise the Value of Work Scale (VW), and items 26 through 31 comprise the Organizational Commitment Scale (OgC). After you have reversed the appropriate items, add together your responses for each group of items to obtain your scores on these four scales.

NORMS

OcC	JI	VW	OgC	PERCENTILE
50	30	32	27	85
47	27	29	25	70
43	24	26	22	50
39	21	23	19	30
36	18	20	17	15

High scores indicate a greater level of the characteristic in question. If, for instance, you received a percentile score of 70 on OcC, it means that 70 percent of people have a lower level of Occupational Commitment than you do.

For more information see G. Blau, A. Paul, and N. St. John, "On Developing a General Index of Work Commitment," *Journal of Vocational Behavior* 42 (1993): 298–314.

ABOUT THE WORK COMMITMENT INDEX

Dr. Gary Blau of Temple University developed the Work Commitment Index for companies that were concerned about retaining their best employees and wanted to gain a greater theoretical understanding of how people feel about work, and how they view their occupation, their specific job, and the organization they work for. The Work Commitment Index is an especially useful instrument to evaluate how you feel about your current work situation.

The meaning of the scores on the four scales is made relatively clear by their labels, but the distinctions among them are important. For instance, the first scale, Occupational Commitment, was defined by Blau as reflecting one's beliefs, feelings, and behavioral intentions about one's chosen occupation; and the second, the Job Involvement Scale, refers to one's beliefs, feelings, and behavioral intentions about a specific job. To illustrate the difference, a stockbroker, for example, may love doing research about the financial prospects of companies and making recommendations to clients about their portfolios but, at the same time, dislike the specific requirements of his or her job. Perhaps our hypothetical stockbroker is required to make several hundred phone calls each week in an attempt to convince strangers to become clients and finds this specific job element distasteful. This person might receive an above average score on the Occupational Commitment Scale but receive a below average score on the Job

Involvement Scale. On the other hand, a person who receives a low score on the Occupational Commitment Scale is almost certain to receive a low score on the Job Involvement Scale. If one does not find an occupation satisfying, it is extremely difficult to find a job within that occupation that would be satisfying.

When taking the Work Commitment Test, it is important to make the distinction between your occupation and your job. I have known a number of people over the years who did not like their jobs but found their occupations satisfying. Most of these people, however, initially concluded that they were dissatisfied with both their jobs *and* their occupations. For instance, Emily was a junior high school science teacher, in the public schools, who came to hate her job after a few years. She said that she spent more time being a disciplinarian than a teacher and that she was tired of parents blaming her for their children's poor grades. When I asked her if she found anything about her job satisfying, she did acknowledge that she thoroughly enjoyed working with the science club, since the students in it were so enthusiastic about learning. After exploring her options over several months, Emily decided to work toward a master's degree. Three years later she was teaching advanced placement classes in a high school, and she found the students' motivation invigorating. If you received low scores on both the Occupational Commitment Scale and the Job Involvement Scale, you may find it useful to retake the test while focusing on the most desirable aspect of your job. Perhaps you do not need to consider a new occupation but, rather, a new job within that occupation.

The third scale on the Work Commitment Index, the Value of Work Scale, is similar to dozens of other tests that have been designed to measure what is called the Protestant work ethic. This ethic is thought to have its origins in an ascetic, Calvinistic brand of Protestantism in which self-denial, self-discipline, hard work, personal honesty, and making productive use of time are highly valued. These theoretical assertions aside, it has been established that people who have a strong Protestant work ethic or, in the case of Blau's scale, a high score on the Value of Work Scale are more likely to be successful in their occupations and earn more money than their low-scoring counterparts. In one study of unemployed young adults, it was found that high scorers were more likely to be employed a year later than were low scorers. Needless to say, employers like applicants who place a high value on work, and several tests of this type are commercially available to personnel directors to use as employee selection tools.

There are two possible explanations if you received a low score on this scale. First, you may not have had the experience of having a job that is right for you. Many young adults (your author included) who had nothing but disdain for those who talked about the importance of work discovered a few years later that they loved their jobs and willingly put in sixty to seventy hours per week. Second, you may be the sort of person who really does not believe that work should be a central focus of one's life. There is certainly nothing wrong with this approach, but it is important that you find a job that allows you to define clearly what your employer can expect of you. You will be very unhappy if you find yourself in a situation in which you are expected to work well into the evening to meet a project deadline.

The final scale on the Work Commitment Index, the Organizational Commitment Scale, was found to be the best predictor of employee turnover. As one can infer from the items, a low score on this scale indicates either indifference toward or alienation from the organization one works for. Your score on this scale would be of more interest to your employer than to you. Companies have distinct organizational climates, and if a majority of employees have a low commitment to the organization, the company will have difficulty retaining its best employees and, consequently, achieving profitability. If you are a manager and you learn that your employees have low scores on this scale, your success will depend in large part on your ability to make your employees feel that they are a part of your organization and to personally involve them in achieving your company's goals. If you received a low score on this scale but high scores on the three other scales, you might want to look for a company that inspires a sense of commitment. You will find your job even more satisfying, and you will probably do better work.

CHAPTER 9

The Stress at Work Scale

For the following items use the 5-point scale below to indicate the degree to which each item describes your feelings about your work.

5 = Describes My Situation Extremely Well
4 = Describes My Situation Well
3 = Describes My Situation Moderately Well
2 = Describes My Situation Somewhat Well
1 = Does Not Describe My Situation

---

* Reprinted with permission of Dr. Jessica Reynolds Jenner.

if it's
no sales → 5

___1___ 1. I am unclear about what is expected of me.

___2___ 2. Others I work with seem unclear about what my job entails.

___4___ 3. People make conflicting demands for my time.

___4___ 4. I lack confidence in my company's top management.

___1___ 5. I get feedback only when my performance is unsatisfactory.

___1___ 6. Decisions that affect me are made above, without my knowledge.

___2___ 7. People I work with don't do their share.

___2___ 8. I am cautious about what I say in meetings.

___4___ 9. I have too much to do and too little time to do it.

___1___ 10. I have differences of opinion with my superiors.

___1___ 11. I have too much supervision.

___1___ 12. I get no personal support from the people I work with.

___2___ 13. I am in a dead-end job.

___1___ 14. I have unsettled conflicts with the people I work with.

___2___ 15. I spend my time fighting fires, not working to a plan.

___1___ 16. There is conflict between my unit and other units.

___1___ 17. I don't get credit or recognition for what I do.

___1___ 18. I have too little supervision.

5 = Describes My Situation Extremely Well; 4 = Describes My Situation Well;
3 = Describes My Situation Moderately Well; 2 = Describes My Situation Somewhat Well;
1 = Does Not Describe My Situation

SCORING

Simply add together your responses for a total score.

NORMS

MEN	WOMEN	PERCENTILE
56	54	85
51	50	70
46	45	50
41	40	30
36	36	15

High scores indicate greater stress. If, for instance, you received a percentile score of 50, it means that half of all people experience less stress at work than you do.

For more information see J. R. Jenner, "A Measure of Chronic Organizational Stress," *Psychological Reports* 58 (1986): 543–46.

ABOUT THE STRESS AT WORK SCALE

Stress is a generic term that can have more than one meaning. One way in which the term is used refers to environmental events. That is, we might say that we work under stressful conditions. A second meaning of the term involves people's reactions to environmental events. We would be using the term in this sense if we were to say, "I'm feeling stressed out." This distinction is important because it can be difficult for those in the midst of a stress attack to determine whether the conditions in which they are working are to blame or their reactions are unnecessarily intense given their circumstances.

It is nearly impossible to develop a test that can distinguish between these two situations. For instance, I would respond with a 5 to item 10 because the administration at my university wants to do away with tenure, increase faculty teaching load, and retain even the most marginal students. I, however, would like to keep both my tenure and my teaching load; and if it were up to me, I would wash out those students who cannot earn C's in their courses even with today's relaxed grading standards. If I did feel "stressed out," would that mean my working environment is stressful or that I am overreacting to the circumstances?

I would say the latter, because it is almost always the case that college administrators and college faculty have different goals. I doubt that I could find a university at which administrators see it as their job to help faculty achieve their goals. Most college administrators see it as their job to impose their goals on their faculty.

Perhaps the best method of identifying the relative importance of environmental conditions and personal reactions is to look for consensus. I have a few colleagues, for instance, who do find their jobs extremely stressful, but the majority of us continue to find the atmosphere at work relatively relaxed. So, my conclusion would be that my colleagues who complain about their stressful jobs should consider changing the way in which they view them. The environmental stresses are no greater than they are at any typical university.

If you received a high score on this test, you must determine whether your workplace is unusually stressful or you are prone to reacting more strongly than others to a job that produces a typically high level of stress. Keep in mind that you will never find a job that does not impose at least some demands that will make you uncomfortable.

If you react more intensely than your colleagues, the work of Dr. Richard Lazarus, a psychologist known for his stress research, is relevant to you. Lazarus has argued that our cognitions, or our thoughts, are critical in determining how we will react to various environmental events. In one experiment he studied the reactions of people who were facing major surgery. One group, identified as repressors, did not seem to worry about it much. When their surgeons attempted to explain the procedure, these people typically said something like, "I don't need to hear all the gory details. Just do what you have to do." A second group of patients, identified as sensitizers, were quite anxious about their surgery and demanded to know exactly what was going to be done. As you might guess, the repressors experienced less pain following their surgery and had fewer postoperative complications than did the sensitizers.

Repression can go a long way toward reducing your stress level. In my case, for instance, I rarely think about my differences of opinion with my dean and provost. Yes, I may get a little worked up when I receive memos that outline their plans, but typically I quickly dismiss them with a shrug and a "what can you expect?" There is nothing I can do to change their views, so my only alternative is to perform my duties as well as I can and hope for the best.

As Lazarus pointed out, however, repression can be overdone. He cited cases of men (women are rarely this foolish) who, in the midst of a heart attack, were intent on proving to themselves that nothing was wrong. Some men simply ignored their symptoms, telling themselves it was only indigestion. Others actually began to exercise vigorously, again to prove that it was nothing serious. Repression in moderation seems to be the most effective strategy. (The following test and discussion will provide you with more ideas as to how to deal with stress.)

If it is likely that most of your colleagues would receive the same high score you did, then it may well be the case that your working environment is unusually stressful. You could, of course, look for a different job, but it may be worth your while to try to induce your company to change. In this day of tight labor markets, management is increasingly responsive to the needs of their employees. They know that if they do not provide a reasonable atmosphere, their best workers will leave, and they will be left with those employees who would have trouble finding another job. So you may well get the results you want if you organize a group of valued employees and present to management your view of the problems and your proposed solutions. Yes, there are managers who will react defensively and make your life even more miserable. But if you are miserable to begin with, the potential gains may greatly outweigh the potential costs. It's worth a try.

CHAPTER 10

The Hardiness Inventory

The following statements reflect feelings and beliefs about one's work and one's activities. Using the guidelines below, indicate the degree to which each statement describes you.

1 = Strongly Disagree
2 = Disagree
3 = Neither Agree nor Disagree
4 = Agree
5 = Strongly Agree

___3___ 1. I plan ahead so that I can avoid problems in the future.

___4___ 2. Much of my time is spent doing things that are not worthwhile.

___4___ 3. I like a schedule that involves frequent changes.

✗ ___4___ 4. When I try hard enough, things turn out right.

___1___ 5. There is no point to working hard, because it benefits only the top levels of management.

___4___ 6. Too much variety in my work makes me unfocused.

___4___ 7. When I have problems, I try not to think about them.

___1___ 8. I look forward to returning to work on Mondays.

___3___ 9. I have little patience for abstract theories. — Depends on who they come from.

___4___ 10. My efforts can lead to changes at work.

___4___ 11. I work hard to accomplish my goals. — use to work harder for that.

___4___ 12. I believe that the "tried and true" is the best approach.

___4___ 13. I can communicate in a way that people listen to me. — Employees yes. Customer not always.

___2___ 14. Most lower level employees are simply used by upper management.

___3___ 15. Laws that jeopardize a person's job should not be passed. Depends

___3___ 16. I am good at getting people to change their minds.

___5___ 17. My daydreams are much more exciting than my reality.

___4___ 18. I love waking up fresh to meet the challenges of the day. would love to

___2___ 19. I have never made a mistake that I could not correct.

___4___ 20. I have a clear sense of what is important to me.

___3___ 21. I like situations in which I do not know what will happen.

___4___ 22. I know when I need help on a difficult task.

___3___ 23. Ordinary work is always boring.

1 = Strongly Disagree; 2 = Disagree; 3 = Neither Agree nor Disagree;
4 = Agree; 5 = Strongly Agree

_2_ 24. Society has an <u>obligation</u> to support people who do their best.

_5_ 25. If someone wants to hurt me, there is little I can do about it.

_5_ 26. I believe that if I do my best at work, it will pay off.

_5_ 27. I find opportunities to learn something new about myself exciting.

_3_ 28. Most of the time when someone gets angry at me, it is something I was helpless to prevent.

_4_ 29. Most of my days seem tedious and dull.   at work ad

_3_ 30. I enjoy it when something interrupts my daily routine.

---

1 = Strongly Disagree; 2 = Disagree; 3 = Neither Agree nor Disagree;
4 = Agree; 5 = Strongly Agree

SCORING

The Hardiness Inventory is comprised of three scales. The items that appear on each scale are found below. To find your scores, add your responses together. Items marked with an asterisk (*) are reverse scored.

Control Scale: 1, 4, 7*, 10, 13, 16, 19, 22, 25*, 28*
Commitment Scale: 2*, 5*, 8, 11, 14*, 17*, 20, 23*, 26, 29*
Challenge Scale: 3, 6*, 9*, 12*, 15*, 18, 21, 24*, 27, 30

NORMS

CONTROL	SCORE COMMITMENT	CHALLENGE	PERCENTILE
39	38	41	85
35	34	37	70
31 30	30 31	(33)	50 —
27	26	29	30
23	22	25	15

High scores indicate greater levels of the relevant cognition. If, for instance, you received a percentile score of 70 on Control, it means that 70 percent of people believe they have less Control than you do.

For more information see S. C. Kobasa, "Stress Resistant Personality," in *The Healing Brain: A Scientific Reader*, edited by R. E. Ornstein and C. Swencionis (Oxford, England: Pergamon Press, 1990).

1   3
4   4
7   2
10   4
13   4
16   3
19   2
22   4
25   1
28   3 / 50

* 2 = 2
* 5   5
  8   1
  11 4
* 14 4
* 17 1
  20 4
* 23 3
  26 5
* 29   2
       / 31

3   4
* 6   2
* 9   3
* 12 2
* 15 3
  18 4
  21 3
* 24 4
  27 5
  30 3 / 33

ABOUT THE HARDINESS INVENTORY

I have two colleagues who react to their jobs in very different ways. The first, I'll call him Jim, cannot wait until the start of the fall semester. He loves it when the campus is crowded with students, and he loves it even more when those students are lined up outside his office door, hoping for just a minute of his time. Jim prides himself on his creativity, and he always has three or four research projects going at a time. To help him with his ambitious program, he typically has several undergraduate and graduate students working with him. Jim rarely leaves his office before eight in the evening, and although his family insists that he take the major holidays off, you can count on finding him at his desk throughout most of Christmas and spring breaks. He is always a little sad when he attends the May graduation ceremonies because he knows that the campus will be relatively deserted for several months and that it will be some time before he can get his research in gear once again.

John, on the other hand, loves May graduation because it means that he can finally relax for a few months. He works every bit as hard as Jim, but he complains about it bitterly. He will tell anyone who will listen that the university places unrealistic demands on the faculty and that he simply cannot teach so many students and continue to be a productive researcher. John also frequently complains of headaches, and in a typical academic year he will miss half a dozen classes as a result of "intestinal problems." John regularly announces the number of years he has left until he can retire.

As the case of Jim and John so vividly illustrates, stress is in the eye of the beholder. Jim loves to be busy. The slow pace of summer vacations leaves him feeling restless and mildly depressed. John on the other hand, luxuriates in his all too brief summer vacation and begins every fall wondering how he can survive another year. Despite John's claims, it is not his demanding schedule that causes him to experience stress; it is the way in which he views his day-to-day activities that is responsible for his headaches and his stomach problems.

Nearly twenty years ago, Dr. Suzanne Kobasa conducted an ambitious study in an attempt to learn how executives coped with stress on the job. When AT&T agreed to break up into several smaller companies in response to pressure from the Justice Department, Kobasa reasoned that the transition would be extremely stressful for the company's management personnel. They would have to face a new set of demands, and they knew that at least some of them would be out of a job once the dust settled. Kobasa administered an extensive battery of tests to the executives and followed the executives through the transition period in an attempt to learn if certain personality characteristics were related to the ability to cope with the extraordinary stress.

She concluded that the three personality characteristics that make up the Hardiness Inventory, often referred to as the three Cs, did serve to insulate the executives from the negative effects of stress.

The Control Scale measure the belief that one can exert control over a situation, that one's efforts do make a difference. Executives who suffered during this period tended to believe that they were the helpless victims of circumstances, that forces beyond their control would determine what happened to them. Those who thrived during the transition were convinced that if they worked hard and smart, they might actually come out ahead once the reorganization was complete.

The Commitment Scale measures the belief that one's work is important and worthwhile. People with a strong sense of commitment enjoy their work; they even find it exciting. They are the kind of people who cannot wait for Monday morning so that they can get back to their desk and meet their responsibilities head-on. Those low on Commitment view their jobs as a somewhat onerous duty. They realize they have to keep at it if they are to put food on their families' tables, but they take little pleasure in anything they might accomplish. People high in Commitment would continue to work after winning the lottery. Low scorers would walk out the door as soon as they learned they had the winning numbers.

The Challenge Scale measures the belief that change is nothing more than a chance to prove one's skills and competence. Executives high on this dimension saw the breakup as an opportunity to shape the destiny of their company and their personal future. They found the changes exciting as well as challenging. Executives with little sense of challenge viewed the changes as an onerous burden they could only endure. They wondered why the Justice Department could not have waited for a few more years until they retired or could find another job. These people crave predictability because for them it represents safety and security.

It is noteworthy that it does not matter which set of beliefs is actually more accurate. For instance, perhaps the executives who had a strong sense of control were really fooling themselves. Perhaps their efforts really did not make a bit of difference. Nonetheless, their belief that they could exert control enabled them to cope and even thrive with the stress that was making their low-scoring colleagues physically ill.

If you received low scores on these three dimensions, you can change your attitudes by making a concerted effort to do so. You cannot, however, use the excuse that you do not really believe that you can exert any control over your destiny or that there is no good reason for you to experience a sense of commitment to your work. You could be right, but you are only hurting yourself by maintaining your cynical attitudes.

It is also likely that by insisting that low scores on these three scales is the more rational way to view the world of work, you are creating a self-fulfilling prophecy. If you insist, for instance, that nothing you do can make a difference, the odds are that you will do nothing to make a difference. The only chance you have to exert control over your career or to experience the satisfaction of doing a job well is to accept the idea that these things are possible. A positive attitude can really work wonders.

Room for Improvement

After taking the tests in this section, you will learn if you have the personal characteristics necessary for a successful career. These are the tests in Part III:

CHAPTER 11

The Fear of Success Scale

In this questionnaire you will find a number of statements that measure personal attitudes. There are no right or wrong answers. Please answer all items using the scale below.

7 = Definitely Disagree
6 = Disagree
5 = Somewhat Disagree
4 = Undecided
3 = Somewhat Agree
2 = Agree
1 = Definitely Agree

* Reprinted with permission of Dr. Miron Zuckerman.

_____ 1. I expect other people to fully appreciate my potential.

_____ 2. Often the cost of success is greater than the reward.

_____ 3. For every winner there are several rejected and unhappy losers.

_____ 4. The only way I can prove my worth is by winning a game or doing well on a task.

_____ 5. I enjoy telling my friends that I have done something especially well.

_____ 6. It is more important to play the game than to win it.

_____ 7. In my attempt to do better than others, I realize I may lose many of my friends.

_____ 8. In competition I try to win no matter what.

_____ 9. A person who is at the top faces nothing but a constant struggle to stay there.

_____ 10. I am happy only when I am doing better than others.

_____ 11. I think success has been emphasized too much in our culture.

_____ 12. In order to achieve one must give up the fun things in life.

_____ 13. The cost of success is overwhelming responsibility.

_____ 14. Achievement commands respect.

_____ 15. I become embarrassed when others compliment me on my work.

_____ 16. A successful person is often considered by others to be both aloof and snobbish.

_____ 17. When you're on top, everyone looks up to you.

_____ 18. People's behavior changes for the worst after they become successful.

_____ 19. When competing against another person, I sometimes feel better if I lose than if I win.

7 = Definitely Disagree; 6 = Disagree; 5 = Somewhat Disagree;
4 = Undecided; 3 = Somewhat Agree; 2 = Agree; 1 = Definitely Agree

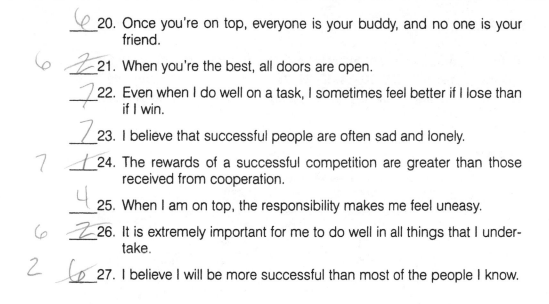

_6_ 20. Once you're on top, everyone is your buddy, and no one is your friend.

6 _7_ 21. When you're the best, all doors are open.

_7_ 22. Even when I do well on a task, I sometimes feel better if I lose than if I win.

_7_ 23. I believe that successful people are often sad and lonely.

7 _1_ 24. The rewards of a successful competition are greater than those received from cooperation.

_4_ 25. When I am on top, the responsibility makes me feel uneasy.

6 _7_ 26. It is extremely important for me to do well in all things that I under-take.

2 _6_ 27. I believe I will be more successful than most of the people I know.

42+9½ = 135

SCORING

Before scoring the Fear of Success Scale, reverse your responses to the following items: 1, 4, 5, 8, 10, 14, 17, 21, 24, 26, and 27. After reversing these items, simply add your responses together to obtain your total score.

NORMS

WOMEN	MEN	PERCENTILE
126	122	85
119	115	70
111	107	50
103	99	30
96	92	15

For more information see M. Zuckerman, and S. N. Allison, "An Objective Measure of Fear of Success: Construction and Validation," *Journal of Personality Assessment* 40 (1976): 422–30.

ABOUT THE FEAR OF SUCCESS SCALE

Fear of success became a hot topic among psychologists in the late 1960s, when Matina Horner published her study indicating that women were especially likely to have strong fears of success. Horner's study was quite simple. She asked college men and women to write a story in response to a lead sentence that read: After first term finals, Anne finds herself at the top of her medical school class. In the sentence that men received, the name Anne was replaced with the name John. Horner's results were nothing short of astounding. Anne did not live happily ever after in a majority of the stories written by women. Some women wrote that Anne was reviled and even tormented by her classmates. Others wrote that Anne had cheated to get to the top of her class and was later consumed with guilt. Still others wrote that Anne was embarrassed by her success and made sure that her name never appeared at the top of the list again. Fully 65 percent of women's stories included these negative themes, which Horner believed were evidence of fear of success. Men, on the other hand, had few problems with finding John's name at the top of the list. Only 9 percent of men wrote stories that reflected fear of success.

Horner's groundbreaking study inspired a flurry of research that continues today, thirty years later. One conclusion that can be drawn from this work is that both men and women are likely to fear success in careers that are typically occupied by people of the other sex. In the 1960s, medicine was dominated by men more so than today, so women perceived success in this field as evidence that their femininity might be lacking. Men, on the other hand, felt comfortable about succeeding as physicians, but they exhibited high levels of fear of success when questioned about vocations such as nurse or dietitian—careers typically filled by women. Men seemed to believe that success in such a career would cast doubts on their masculinity.

The evidence suggests that over the past few decades men and women are becoming more similar in their levels of fear of success. Since it is now much more common to find women in fields such as medicine and law than it was thirty years ago, these women are not as likely to perceive success in these disciplines as a threat to their femininity. It remains the case, however, that both men and women who subscribe to traditional sex roles are more likely to experience fear of success than people with nontraditional attitudes. Those of you (especially women) who received a high score on this scale might find it useful to ask yourself if you are limiting your options as a result of your views about the proper roles for men and women. Being a successful doctor or attorney need not make a woman less feminine, nor does being a successful editor or elementary school teacher make a man less masculine.

The clearest danger of fear of success is that it can prevent people from trying their best. People with this fear believe, whether they articulate it or not, that success results in a variety of consequences—none of them good. They believe that successful people are not liked by others, that they tend to have unhappy personal lives, and that they have to exploit others to achieve their success. So some very talented people may perform below their capabilities so as to blend in with the crowd. The thought of being identified as valedictorian or employee of the year is quite frightening to these people. These concerns are impossible to understand by many of us who would love the recognition, but those with strong fears of success are likely to have vague suspicions that this recognition will result in personal pain.

A recent study by Drs. Scott Wallace and Lynn Alden of the University of British Columbia found a very interesting difference between people who did and people who did not have fears of success. They asked college men and women to perform a task and arranged the situation so that success was inevitable. The men and women who had a fear of success exhibited a negative emotional reaction to their experience. Their first thought seemed to be "Now people will expect even more of me in the future." The researchers made the point that interpreting successful experiences in this negative way makes it very difficult for such people to ever revise their self-images in such a way that they might come to enjoy and value success.

Another characteristic of those who have this fear is that even when they do experience success, they cannot feel comfortable with it. They believe that their success was a fluke, that they happened to get lucky. Because they did not deserve their success, they fear that others will discover they are not really capable or competent after all and that eventually they will have to face the humiliation of being exposed as an impostor. The end result is that they resolve never to make the mistake of bringing attention to themselves again by being successful.

The one encouraging thing about fear of success is that it does diminish with time as long as people do not give in to it. I remember a time that I felt extremely embarrassed when my instructor identified me as having the highest score on a statistics exam. I did not make a conscious decision at the time to avoid a similar humiliation again, but then I never did receive the highest score on subsequent exams. With the advantage of lots of hindsight, I cannot help but conclude that my academic career could have been more successful had I not suffered from fear of success.

Despite my feelings of discomfort, I continued with school, and I continued to try to do the things that symbolized success in my field. It was a gradual change, but I have reached the point now where I feel confident that I could luxuriate in a major success. Indeed, I wouldn't mind if you put me to the test by doing what you could to get this book on the bestseller list.

If you did have a high score on this scale, you can speed up the process of reducing your fears by directly challenging your beliefs. To do this, take a close look at the items on the test. Item 3, for instance, suggests that if you win, there must be other people who lose. Well, this simply is not true. If my book does make it to the bestseller list, it does not mean that I am preventing anyone else from writing a well-received book. If you receive a perfect score on a final exam, you are not preventing other students from doing the same. If you become an exceptionally competent physician or attorney, you are not preventing others from doing the same.

Life provides us with endless lessons that help us to accept the idea that success can be gratifying, but you can hasten the process by giving up your negative beliefs about the consequences of success. Give it a try. Don't back away from it, and I guarantee that within a few years you will enjoy striving to be the best that you can be.

CHAPTER 12

The Achievement Motive Scale

The following items consist of a sentence stem and several alternative ways of completing the sentence. Your task is to decide which alternative best describes you. Place an *X* by the alternative that best describes you.

* Reprinted with permission of Dr. Hubert J. M. Hermans.

1. Working is something that

    ＿＿＿＿ I would rather not do.

    ＿＿＿＿ I don't like doing very much.

    ＿＿＿＿ I would rather do now and then.

    ＿＿＿＿ I like doing.

    ＿＿＿＿ I like doing very much.

2. At school they thought I was

    ＿＿＿＿ very diligent.

    ＿＿＿＿ diligent.

    ＿＿＿＿ not always so diligent.

    ＿＿＿＿ rather easygoing.

    ＿＿＿＿ very easygoing.

3. Other people think I

    ＿＿＿＿ work very hard.

    ＿＿＿＿ work hard.

    ＿＿＿＿ work pretty hard.

    ＿＿＿＿ don't work very hard.

    ＿＿＿＿ don't work hard.

4. To prepare yourself a long time for an important task

    ＿＿＿＿ really is senseless.

    ＿＿＿＿ often is rather rash.

    ＿＿＿＿ can often be useful.

    ＿＿＿＿ testifies to a sense of reality.

    ＿＿＿＿ is necessary to succeed.

5. When I am working, the demands I make upon myself are

____ very high.

____ high.

____ pretty high.

____ not so high.

____ low.

____ very low.

6. When the teacher gave lessons at school,

____ I usually set my heart on doing my best and making a favorable impression.

____ I usually paid great attention to the things being said.

____ my thoughts often strayed to other things.

____ I was more interested in things that had nothing to do with school.

7. I usually do

____ much more than I resolved to do.

____ a bit more than I resolved to do.

____ a little less than I resolved to do.

____ much less than I resolved to do.

8. If I have not attained my goal and have not done a task well,

____ I continue to do my best to attain the goal.

____ I exert myself once again to attain the goal.

____ I find it difficult to not lose heart.

____ I'm inclined to give up.

____ I usually give up.

9. At high school I thought perseverance was

____ very unimportant.

____ rather unimportant.

____ important.

____ very important.

10. To begin homework was

____ a very great effort.

____ a great effort.

____ a rather great effort.

____ not much effort.

____ very little effort.

11. When I was in high school, the standards I set for myself with regard to my studies were

____ very high.

____ average.

____ low.

____ very low.

12. If I was called from my homework to watch television or listen to the radio, then afterward

____ I always went straight back to work.

____ I would only take a short pause and then go back to work.

____ I would always wait a little before starting again.

____ I would find it very difficult to begin again.

13. Work that requires great responsibility

____ I would like to do very much.

____ I would only do if I was paid well.

____ I don't think I would be capable of doing.

____ is completely unattractive to me.

14. I would find a life in which one wouldn't have to work at all

    ____ ideal.

    ____ very pleasant.

    ____ pleasant.

    ____ unpleasant.

    ____ very unpleasant.

15. When I was in high school, I thought that to attain a high position in society was

    ____ unimportant.

    ____ of little importance.

    ____ not so important.

    ____ rather important.

    ____ very important.

16. When doing something difficult,

    ____ I give it up very quickly.

    ____ I give it up quickly.

    ____ I give it up rather quickly.

    ____ I don't give up too soon.

    ____ I usually see it through.

17. In general I am

    ____ very strongly future oriented.

    ____ strongly future oriented.

    ____ not so strongly future oriented.

    ____ not at all future oriented.

18. At school I found classmates who studied very hard

    _____ very nice.

    _____ nice.

    _____ just as nice as others who didn't work as hard.

    _____ not nice.

    _____ not nice at all.

19. At school I admired persons who had reached a very high position in life

    _____ very much.

    _____ much.

    _____ little.

    _____ not at all.

20. For life's extra pleasures

    _____ I usually have no time.

    _____ I often have no time.

    _____ I sometimes have too little time.

    _____ I usually have enough time.

    _____ I always have time.

21. I usually am

    _____ very busy.

    _____ busy.

    _____ not busy.

    _____ not busy at all.

22. I can work at something without getting tired for

    ____   a very long time.

    ____   a long time.

    ____   not too long a time.

    ____   only a short time.

    ____   only a very short time.

23. Good relations with my teachers at high school

    ____   were appreciated very much.

    ____   were appreciated.

    ____   were thought not to be so important.

    ____   were thought to be exaggerated in value.

    ____   were thought to be completely unimportant.

24. Children succeed their parents as managers of the family business because

    ____   they want to enlarge and extend the business.

    ____   they are lucky their parents are managers.

    ____   they can put their new views into practice.

    ____   this is the easiest way to earn money.

25. When I was in high school, I was

    ____   extremely ambitious.

    ____   very ambitious.

    ____   not so ambitious.

    ____   a little ambitious.

    ____   hardly ambitious at all.

26. Organizing something is something

_____   I like doing very much.

_____   I like doing.

_____   I don't like doing very much.

_____   I don't like doing at all.

27. When I begin something, I

_____   never carry it to a successful conclusion.

_____   seldom carry it to a successful conclusion.

_____   sometimes carry it to a successful conclusion.

_____   usually carry it to a successful conclusion.

_____   always carry it to a successful conclusion.

28. I

_____   very often am bored.

_____   often am bored.

_____   sometimes am bored.

_____   hardly ever am bored.

_____   never am bored.

29. Shopping is something

_____   I like very much.

_____   I like.

_____   I don't like.

_____   I hate.

SCORING

The format of this test makes scoring somewhat complicated. For each item, the alternatives count from one to six points. To find out how many points your response was worth, you will have to number the alternatives sequentially. For some items, such as the first one, the numbering begins with the first alternative. So, for example, "I would rather not do" is worth one point, "I don't like doing very much" is worth two points, and "I like doing very much," accordingly, is worth five points. For other items, such as the second one, the sequential numbering begins with the last alternative. So, for the second item, the final alternative, "very easygoing," is worth one point, "rather easygoing" is worth two points, and "very diligent," accordingly, is worth five points. The following guide indicates whether you begin the sequential numbering of the alternative with the first one or the last one. After you have assigned numbers to all the alternatives, find the total of your selections.

1.	First	16.	First
2.	Last	17.	Last
3.	Last	18.	Last
4.	First	19.	Last
5.	Last	20.	Last
6.	Last	21.	Last
7.	Last	22.	Last
8.	Last	23.	Last
9.	First	24.	Last
10.	First	25.	Last
11.	Last	26.	Last
12.	Last	27.	First
13.	Last	28.	First
14.	First	29.	Last
15.	First		

NORMS

SCORE	PERCENTILE
112	85
106	70
100	50
94	30
88	15

(I would like to thank Lek Wanichtanom for her help in developing these norms.)

For more information see H. J. M. Hermans, "A Questionnaire Measure of Achievement Motivation," *Journal of Applied Psychology* 54 (1970): 353–63.

ABOUT THE ACHIEVEMENT MOTIVE SCALE

The achievement motive has a rich history in psychology. It has been studied by numerous researchers throughout this century, but perhaps this important motive is most closely associated with the work of Harvard psychologist David McClelland. During the 1950s and 1960s, McClelland published a substantial body of research detailing how young children acquire the motive to achieve, how it affects the behavior of various groups of people ranging from children to college students to business people, and how adults deficient in their achievement motivation can acquire this integral ingredient for success.

McClelland experimented with a variety of methods for measuring the achievement motive before concluding that the most effective method was the use of a rather cumbersome test called the Thematic Apperception Test, widely known as the TAT. It requires people to tell stories to a series of pictures. Their stories are transcribed verbatim and then scored for achievement themes by trained judges. While this technique produced good results, it was not very efficient. The test you just completed, developed by Dr. Hubert Hermans of the University of Nijmegen in the Netherlands, was one of the first self-report tests that measured the achievement motive as well as and perhaps even more effectively than the TAT. So, the results of this test should provide you with a good indication of whether you have sufficient drive to achieve the success you desire or, for those of you who scored below the 50th percentile, whether it might be worth your while to work on increasing your achievement motivation.

Hermans selected items for his test to reflect what researchers believe are the essential components of the achievement motive. The first component, and the one that has received the most attention, is aspiration level. People high in achievement motivation prefer tasks at the intermediate difficulty level. They have little patience with easy tasks, even when success means winning an attractive prize, because such tasks do not present a challenge. Nor do they like impossibly difficult tasks, because they conclude that success would be more a matter of luck than their skill and effort. They like tasks that are difficult enough to be challenging yet allow for the possibility that their skills and efforts will result in success.

Risk taking and persistence are two interrelated components of the achievement motive. People high in achievement motivation shy away from tasks that involve a high degree of risk. If asked to perform a task that has a very low probability of success, they tend to give up rather quickly. On the other hand, high scorers are extremely persistent on tasks for which there is about a fifty-fifty chance of success. People high in achievement motivation seem to want to tackle tasks for which there is a reasonable chance of success, and they are willing to keep at such tasks until they do succeed. They simply do not like wasting their time on tasks that offer very little chance of success.

People high in achievement motivation view time differently than do low scorers. The high scorers view time as dynamic, as a quantity that is fleeting, one that passes all too quickly. High scorers are also more future oriented. They can project the consequences of their actions and are willing to take a long-term view of their efforts.

Finally, those high in achievement motivation have a definite preference when it comes to colleagues. They want competent partners and are not especially concerned with interpersonal qualities. Low scorers value characteristics such as agreeableness and capacity to be sympathetic over competence in their choice of partners.

Given these characteristics, it should not be surprising to learn that people high in achievement motivation are likely to exhibit upward mobility. They tend to achieve higher levels of occupational status than do their parents. Low scorers, on the other hand, tend to have the same occupational status as their parents and may even fall a step or two below.

What can you do if you received a low score on this test? As I previously hinted, McClelland developed a program to train low scorers to develop the motivation to achieve. While his program is quite intensive, the principles are actually quite simple and straightforward. Let us briefly review his program. For those of you who would like more complete information, many public libraries and most college libraries have copies of his books.

First, McClelland asked participants to take his test in the way a person high in achievement motivation would. You can accomplish this by going back through Hermans's test and reading the responses, preferably several times, that would yield the maximum score. Obviously, you cannot change the past, but this step will familiarize you with the way a person high in achievement motivation views the world.

Second, you must link changes in attitude with changes in behavior. For instance, item 3 suggests that you make an effort to give others reason to see you as a person who works very hard. As a second example, you could use item 17 to develop a plan for your future. You could begin by writing down where you would like to be five years from now and working back to the present from that point. You might decide that to get there, you have to finish your degree or complete a specialized training program within two years.

Third, you must learn to accept your new achievement orientation as an improvement in your self-image. McClelland encouraged his trainees to engage in an honest self-appraisal. To emphasize the point that not everyone can feel comfortable with the idea of becoming achievement oriented, he would tell the story of a trainee who, during this phase of the program, decided that he did not want to become such a person. This man left the program and resigned from his management position to become a chicken farmer. Most people, though, can see the advantages of developing motivation to achieve and come to like this new side of themselves.

Finally, you are required to write an essay describing your plan for the next two years. Be sure to describe your future realistically and to set goals that are moderately difficult to achieve.

The remaining elements of McClelland's program are designed to increase the odds that participants will follow through with the changes they have made and to promote the adoption of their new identity as a high need-for- achievement person. You can do this on your own. Regularly review your goals and the progress you have made toward achieving them. Revise your goals, as necessary, as you go along. And continue to remind yourself of the benefits of becoming such a person. Yes, one element of these benefits is material; people high in the achievement motive are more successful than low scorers. But the most important benefit will be your ability to feel good about yourself and to take pride in knowing that you have made your very best effort.

CHAPTER 13

The Procrastination Scale

The following statements describe people's reactions to a variety of situations. Please respond to each item using the following 4-point scale.

4 = That's me for sure.
3 = That's my tendency.
2 = That's not my tendency.
1 = That's not me for sure.

* Reprinted with permission of Dr. Bruce W. Tuckman, Florida State University.

_____ 1. I needlessly delay finishing jobs, even when they're important.

_____ 2. I postpone starting in on things I don't like to do.

_____ 3. When I have a deadline, I wait till the last minute.

_____ 4. I delay making tough decisions.

_____ 5. I stall on initiating new activities.

_____ 6. I'm on time for appointments.

_____ 7. I keep putting off improving my work habits.

_____ 8. I get right to work, even on life's unpleasant chores.

_____ 9. I manage to find an excuse for not doing something.

_____10. I avoid doing those things that I expect to do poorly.

_____11. I put the necessary time into even boring tasks, like studying.

_____12. When I get tired of an unpleasant job, I stop.

_____13. I believe in "keeping my nose to the grindstone."

_____14. When something's not worth the trouble, I stop.

_____15. I believe that things I do not like doing should not exist.

_____16. I consider people who make me do unfair and difficult things to be rotten.

_____17. When it counts, I can manage to enjoy even studying.

_____18. I am an incurable time waster.

_____19. I feel that it's my absolute right to have other people treat me fairly.

_____20. I believe that other people don't have the right to give me deadlines.

_____21. Studying makes me feel entirely miserable.

_____22. I'm a time waster now, but I can't seem to do anything about it.

_____23. When something's too tough to tackle, I believe in postponing it.

---

4 = That's me for sure; 3 = That's my tendency;
2 = That's not my tendency; 1 = That's not me for sure.

____24. I promise myself I'll do something and then drag my feet.

____25. Whenever I make a plan of action, I follow it.

____26. I wish I could find an easy way to get myself moving.

____27. When I have trouble with a task, it's usually my own fault.

____28. Even though I hate myself if I don't get started, it doesn't get me going.

____29. I always finish important jobs with time to spare.

____30. When I'm done with my work, I check it over.

____31. I look for a loophole or shortcut to get through a tough task.

____32. I get stuck in neutral even though I know how important it is to get started.

____33. I never met a job I couldn't "lick."

____34. Putting something off until tomorrow is not the way I do it.

____35. I feel that work burns me out.

4 = That's me for sure; 3 = That's my tendency;
2 = That's not my tendency; 1 = That's not me for sure.

SCORING

Before you add your scores together, you must reverse score (i.e., 4 = 1, 3 = 2, 2 = 3, 1 = 4) the following items: 6, 8, 11, 13, 17, 25, 29, 30, 33, 34.

NORMS

SCORE	PERCENTILE
106	85
97	70
88	50
79	30
70	15

High scores indicate a greater level of procrastination. If, for instance, you received a percentile score of 70, this means that 70 percent of people have less of a tendency to procrastinate than you do.

For more information see B. W. Tuckman, "The Development and Concurrent Validity of the Procrastination Scale," *Educational and Psychological Measurement* 51 (1991): 473–80.

ABOUT THE PROCRASTINATION SCALE

Procrastination is more than simply the thief of time; it is a serious roadblock to having a successful career. Successful people are doers who take the initiate and make things happen. Procrastinators, of course, have the best intentions of doing it tomorrow, but before they know it, they run out of tomorrows. The good news is that while a very destructive habit, procrastination can be reduced if one makes a well-planned effort to change. If you received a score above the 50th percentile, read this section very carefully.

Florida State University psychologist Bruce Tuckman based his scale on the assumption that procrastination results from a combination of three factors. The first is a disbelief in one's capability to perform some task. I have seen a number of people in psychotherapy over the years who sought help because they could not seem to take the steps they knew were necessary to achieve success in their careers. As one example, Sam was a high school English teacher who wanted to be a full-time writer. He knew he had the ability because several of his college professors encouraged him to write. But while he had been collecting notes for his novel for years, he had not written so much as a single page. On those increasingly rare occasions when he did sit down with good intentions in front of his keyboard, he would think of one last task he had to attend to before he could write with a clear mind.

The second factor is an inability to delay gratification. To illustrate, Elaine dropped out of college after two years and obtained a good job as a debugger with a software development company. She soon began to find her job tedious and became increasingly frustrated because she knew she had more programming ability than many of the software engineers she worked with. She came to realize that she had to obtain her degree if she wanted a chance at a promotion. But she could not bring herself to make the necessary sacrifices to save money for tuition, nor could she face the prospect of giving up several of her evenings each week. Four years later, she was still telling herself that "next semester the time will be right for me to go back to school."

The third factor identified by Tuckman is assigning blame for one's "predicament" to external sources. Evan was a commercial artist for an advertising company; he wanted to become a project manager. He knew other commercial artists who had made the transition, but he could not force himself to take the initiative in the same way his colleagues had. His lament was "It wouldn't make any difference. My supervisors wouldn't give me a fair chance."

The first step to changing your procrastinating ways is to identify your reason for inaction. It may not fall neatly into a single category, so consider the possibility that two and possibly all three of these factors may play a role in your procrastination.

If you see yourself in either the first or the second category, the second step is to break down your goals into smaller segments. After several hours of therapy, Sam acknowledged that he was not sure he had the ability to write the six hundred pages it would take to make a novel. And even if he could write six hundred pages, he complained that he did not know if it would be any good. I asked him if he could write one high-quality page. "Of course I can," he replied, somewhat testily. The following week he brought in eight pages he could offer as evidence. Ten months later he was sending his novel to agents. While waiting for a response, he was beginning to work on his second book.

Elaine could not make the decision to go back to school; in her mind it had to be an all-or-none proposition. She said that if she were to go back, she would want to get it over with as quickly as possible; this meant attending classes four nights each week and a tuition bill of nearly $1,500. Her first assignment was to call the local university and ask them to send her a class schedule for the following semester. It took her two weeks to complete this simple task, but within a month she had registered for one programming course—for which, she learned, her company was willing to pay half the tuition. For the following two semesters she also registered for a single course, but once she could see her goal in sight, her motivation increased dramatically. She quit her job and, with the help of student loans, completed her degree in fifteen months. Today she is earning three times as much as her previ-

ous salary, and she loves the challenge presented by every project she directs.

Most tasks that lead to career advancement, when considered as a whole, seem either overwhelming or to require too large a sacrifice. But it is almost always possible to break down these tasks into steps small enough that even the worst procrastinator can manage. And keep in mind that the alternative to taking that first small step is to stagnate in your career.

People who fall into the third category often have difficulty recognizing themselves. So, if at first blush you conclude that "blaming others" is not something you do, take a moment to reflect on your situation.

I think the comic strip "Dilbert" serves as a good projective test for such people. I have met a number of dissatisfied people who love to compare notes about Dilbert's inept manager. These people identify closely with Dilbert and his friend Wally and comfort each other with mutual assurances that their own career progress has been stifled by management that either does not recognize their talents or fails to provide them with the opportunities to demonstrate them. I do find Dilbert amusing, and I see a number of parallels between his pointy-haired manager and the administrators I work for. But, on the other hand, I feel annoyed at real-life Dilberts for failing to do anything about their less than ideal situations. I want to tell them to look for other jobs, start their own businesses, upgrade their skills, do anything except blame someone else for their troubles.

It is true that some people are more fortunate than others when it comes to having helpful and encouraging mentors. But in the final analysis, we are all responsible for our lots in life. If you are unhappy with your career progress, you only have yourself to blame. As soon as you put this book down, take out a pencil and paper and begin listing the steps you could take to get your career on track. You have nothing to lose and a great deal to gain.

CHAPTER 14

The Creativity Questionnaire

Read each of the following questions carefully. If your answer to the question is yes, indicate this with a *1*. If your answer to the question is no, indicate this with a *0*.

_____ 1. Are you an only child?

_____ 2. Do you prefer to be an individual contributor as opposed to a team member?

_____ 3. Do you participate in team sports such as baseball, football, basketball, or hockey?

_____ 4. Do you like to fish, sail, or hike?

_____ 5. Do you think of yourself as creative?

_____ 6. Are you a first child?

_____ 7. Are you original?

_____ 8. Do you engage in many social activities?

_____ 9. Did you know what you wanted to be before your junior year in college?

_____10. Would you say that you work best with words?

_____11. Do you tend to think in terms of visual problems?

_____12. Do you prefer to work with simple problems?

_____13. Do you do a great deal of reading?

_____14. Did you find your school experiences challenging?

_____15. Can you use tools skillfully?

_____16. Were you usually above the median in school performance?

_____17. Did you ever consider law enforcement as a career?

_____18. Did your parents strongly influence your choice of a career?

_____19. Are you interested in administrative work?

_____20. Do you go to the movies very often?

_____21. Have you ever seriously considered running for political office?

SCORING

Several items are reverse scored. For these items, if you responded with a *1*, change your response to a *0*. If you responded with a *0*, change your response to a *1*. The reverse scored items are 1, 3, 4, 6, 7, 8, 9, 10, 13, 14, 17, 18, 19, 20, and 21. After you have completed this, add the numbers together to find your total score.

NORMS

SCORE	PERCENTILE
15	85
12	70
9	50
6	30
3	15

High scores indicate greater creativity. If, for example, your percentile score was 85, it means that 85 percent of people are less creative than you are.

For more information see B. O. Bergum, "Selection of Specialized Creators," *Psychological Reports* 33 (1973): 635–39.

ABOUT THE CREATIVITY QUESTIONNAIRE

Creativity seems like one of those qualities that is always good to have. But, as Dr. Bruce Bergum of Texas A&M points out, this is not necessarily so. Yes, there are many jobs in which creativity is essential. Research scientists who are searching for new pharmaceutical compounds, advertising executives who are charged with developing a new campaign, or even small business owners who want to find a unique niche in the market must possess a high level of creativity if they are to succeed. On the other hand, highly creative people do not do well in many other jobs. Administrators and real estate appraisers will probably be more successful if they have high levels of persistence and the ability to attend to detail. Indeed, accountants may get into trouble if they are too creative.

In the development of his Creativity Questionnaire, Dr. Bergum set for himself a formidable task. He wanted a test that would not only distinguish inventors/creators from administrators but also distinguish inventors/creators from research analysts as well. The latter is extremely difficult because all scientists have a great deal in common, regardless of whether their focus is contributing to knowledge that leads to new products or performing the painstaking analysis that converts new ideas into viable products. Both types are highly intelligent and well educated and, as part of their graduate training, had to make at least one contribution to original scientific knowledge. The data collected by Dr. Bergum illustrates this problem

well. On item 16, for instance, 100 percent of the research inventors/creators as well as 100 percent of the research analysts said that they were above the median in school performance. Only slightly more than half of the administrators indicated that this was true for them (reinforcing one stereotype we college faculty have of administrators). Also, none of either group of scientists indicated that they had ever considered a career in law enforcement (item 17). Interestingly, nearly half of the administrators had considered such a career (reinforcing a second stereotype about college administrators). As a final example, all of both groups of scientists said yes to item 5, indicating that they thought of themselves as creative people. Needless to say, it is very difficult to distinguish between two groups of people who think of themselves in such similar ways.

It is fascinating to note that several of the items that worked best in distinguishing between the inventors and the analysts do not appear to have much to do with creativity. For instance, on item 8, none of the inventors said that they engaged in many social activities while 62 percent of the analysts said that they did. Also, on item 10, only 12 percent of the inventors said they worked best with words while 62 percent of the analysts said that they did. Bergum concluded that those high in creativity tend to be less verbal and less social than others.

The norms provided here are for workers in general. The average score for Bergum's sample of inventors and creators was 14. So a score near the 85th percentile suggests that you have the potential to be successful in an occupation that requires a high level of creativity.

There are two thoughts that are important to keep in mind about creativity. First, it can be very difficult to really know if one is a creative person. As Bergum's results indicated, many people, with little or no evidence, think of themselves as creative people. If you think of yourself as a creative person and plan to enter a field in which creativity is important but you received a low score on this test, you may be wise to keep your options open. It is true that a low score on the Creativity Questionnaire certainly does not preclude success in such occupations. After all, half of Bergum's inventors received scores below 14. But the reality is that many people who think of themselves as creative do not have what it takes to make original contributions over the long run. Their strengths, equally valuable, may lie in fields such as administration, sales, analysis, or production.

Second, if you do not think of yourself as a creative person but you received a high score on this test, it may be the case that you do not have enough experience or knowledge to make such a judgment. In my twenty-five years of experience with graduate students, I have come to the conclusion that it is very difficult to predict which students will go on to have productive research careers. I have seen students begin their training confident that they would eventually make numerous important contributions to the field, yet they accepted administrative or applied positions upon graduation and never published a single scientific article. On the other hand, one of my most unforgettable students has gone on to have a brilliant research career, even though when he entered our program he was convinced he would never be able to think of an idea for a masters thesis. Kevin came to Old Dominion University with a degree in history, and he later told me that he did not think he would make it through the first semester. Psychology was completely new to him, and he was both shocked and distressed to learn that he was required to take several rigorous courses in statistics. But Kevin persevered and, during his second semester, asked me if he could help with my research. Before the semester was finished, he had completed my study and conducted a second follow-up study completely on his own. Before he completed his Ph.D., Kevin had published half a dozen scientific articles, and he has not slowed down since.

The point is that Kevin was not able to appreciate his extraordinary level of creativity until he had sufficient knowledge of the field and could see what research needed to be done. Despite what many people believe, ideas usually do not come to those who wander aimlessly through the desert waiting for inspiration. Ideas come to those who study their discipline and work hard to master their fields. As Edison said, genius is 99 percent perspiration and one percent inspiration. So, high scorers who do not consider themselves to be creative would be wise to keep open the possibility of pursuing a career that demands this quality. As you learn more about your field, you may surprise yourself with all of your new ideas.

CHAPTER 15

The Computer Attitudes Scale

This instrument is designed to measure attitudes toward the use of computers in our society. It is not a test, so there are no right or wrong answers. Using the scale below, indicate your level of agreement or disagreement in the space that is next to each statement.

5 = Strongly Agree
4 = Agree
3 = Undecided
2 = Disagree
1 = Strongly Disagree

---

* Reprinted with permission of Dr. Gary S. Nickell.

____ 1. Computers will never replace human life.

____ 2. Computers make me uncomfortable because I don't understand them.

____ 3. People are becoming slaves to computers.

____ 4. Computers are responsible for many of the good things we enjoy.

____ 5. Soon our lives will be controlled by computers.

____ 6. I feel intimidated by computers.

____ 7. There are unlimited possibilities of computer applications.

____ 8. The overuse of computers may be harmful and damaging to humans.

____ 9. Computers are dehumanizing to society.

____10. Computers can eliminate a lot of tedious work for people.

____11. The use of computers is enhancing our standard of living.

____12. Computers turn people into just another number.

____13. Computers are lessening the importance of too many jobs now done by humans.

____14. Computers are a fast and efficient means of gaining information.

____15. Computers intimidate me because they seem so complex.

____16. Computers will replace the need for working human beings.

____17. Computers are bringing us into a bright new era.

____18. Soon our world will be completely run by computers.

____19. Life will be easier and faster with computers.

____20. Computers are difficult to understand and frustrating to work with.

---

5 = Strongly Agree; 4 = Agree; 3 = Undecided;
2 = Disagree; 1 = Strongly Disagree

SCORING

The following items are reverse scored (i.e., 5 = 1, 4 = 2, etc.): 2, 3, 5, 6, 8, 9, 12, 13, 15, 16, 18, and 20. After performing these transformations, add together your scores for all twenty items.

NORMS

MEN	WOMEN	PERCENTILE
86	83	85
81	78	70
76	73	50
71	68	30
66	63	15

High scores indicate more favorable attitudes toward computers. If, for example, you received a percentile score of 70, it means that 70 percent of people have less favorable attitudes toward computers than you do.

For more information see G. S. Nickell and J. N. Pinto, "The Computer Attitude Scale," *Computers in Human Behavior* 2 (1987): 301–6.

ABOUT THE COMPUTER ATTITUDES SCALE

As I stated earlier, I believe that for the ambitious and hard working, there are more opportunities today than ever before. One very important reason for this are the advances in computer technology. Computers not only have created an entire new category of highly paid professionals over the past generation but also have made it possible for people in virtually all occupations to be more productive and efficient. We have all heard stories about the countless twenty-somethings who became millionaires in a matter of months after one good idea, but the influence of computers goes far beyond that. Auto mechanics, plumbers, electricians, and carpenters, to name but a few examples, who are unable to utilize computer technology will have a difficult time competing with their colleagues who can. Even in my profession, psychology, computers have had an incredible impact. When I finished graduate school in the early 1970s, personal computers did not exist. But today it is nearly impossible to conduct the research necessary to be awarded tenure without being computer literate. And my colleagues in private practice have either adapted or perished. Both professional activities (e.g., administering psychological tests) and business aspects (e.g., filing insurance forms) demand a high level of computer expertise.

Dr. Gary Nickell of Moorhead State University and Dr. John Pinto of Morningside College are among several researchers who have recognized the importance of attitudes toward computers in achieving occupational success. They developed their Computer Attitude Scale to help identify those individuals with negative attitudes toward computers. Nickell and Pinto argued that such people could benefit from specialized training programs that not only increased their specific computer skills but also helped them view computers in a more favorable light. Simply providing people with computer training may not be sufficient. If they retain their negative attitudes toward the technology, people are still likely to fail. As evidence supporting their position, Nickell and Pinto found that scores on their scale could predict grades in a college introductory computer class. Clearly, people who begin their training with negative attitudes toward computers will not learn as much as those who begin with a positive attitude. Furthermore, these researchers found a very strong, positive correlation between scores on their scale and job performance ratings for a group of computer operators. Given this finding, it is safe to say that those employees with a positive attitude toward computers are the ones who are most likely to receive promotions and pay increases. Attitudes do make a difference.

Nickell and Pinto's research confirmed what most of us already know or at least suspected—that women and older people tend to have more negative attitudes toward computers than do men or younger employees. I knew one woman in her early fifties who retired from a comfortable job earlier than she should have because she refused to learn how to use a word processing program. And while I know a number of women who are both skilled and comfortable with computers, it is clearly the case that my women students (who, by the way, receive higher grades—so it is not a matter of ability) are more likely than men to complain about being unable to complete assignments on time because of computer problems. This is more than an interesting observation. It means that women and older workers who are reluctant to give up their negative attitudes toward computers are at a distinct disadvantage in the job market.

What can you do to improve your attitudes if you received a score below the 50th percentile on the Computer Attitude Scale? First, make an effort to change the way you look at computer technology. As an example, my wife, Meredith, and I have very different views of computers. Meredith complains, for instance, that when she calls a business, she can never talk to a real person. I have had my share of experiences in which I felt trapped in the maze of a poorly designed voice interactive system (called voice mail jail by those who design such systems), but I appreciate what such systems allow me to do. I can call my bank at any hour and learn the balance in my checking account and whether a specific check has been cashed. After the stock market has a good day, I enjoy calling T. Rowe Price to learn what effect this has had on my retirement funds. Meredith has also conveniently forgotten all the times when she was able to talk to a "real person" and was transferred from department to department without ever finding the person she wanted to talk to. As one final example, I remember the days when it was

almost impossible to make it through the checkout line at the grocery store without having to wait for up to ten minutes for a "price check" on an item that the stocking clerk failed to label. With the introduction of bar code scanners, my kids have probably never heard the term *price check*.

Learning to appreciate how computers have made your life more convenient may be a small step, but it is a critical one. If you are to develop more positive attitudes toward computers, you must accentuate the good and minimize the bad.

The second and more difficult step is to become knowledgeable about what computers can do for you. I do not mean to pick on my wife, but she does provide a great example. Meredith must use a computer in her work as a real estate appraiser, but she has never been able to view this as more than a mixed blessing. She learned enough fundamentals of her software program to accomplish her task, but she has no interest in learning the advanced features of her program that would make her work even easier. Her antipathy toward computers is great enough that she has declined to attend any of the workshops that would allow her to learn these features.

With the hope that I have more influence with you than I do with my wife, I encourage you to be open to learning all that you can. Attend classes or workshops and view them as an opportunity rather than as an onerous obligation. If you can remain open to the possibilities, it will make your work easier and make you a more valued employee. The computer age is here. As the Borg are wont to say, resistance is futile.

CHAPTER 16

The Management Style Survey

The following statements describe ways in which managers interact with those working for them. Using the guidelines below, indicate the degree to which these statements describe your interactions with your colleagues. If you have not had experience as a supervisor, imagine how you would respond in such a situation.

1 = Very Much Unlike Me
2 = Somewhat Unlike Me
3 = Neither Like or Unlike Me
4 = Somewhat Like Me
5 = Very Much Like Me

---

* This scale was developed to reflect the work of Dr. Warren Bennis.

____ 1. I pay close attention to what my supervisees have to say when we are talking.

____ 2. I try my best to be clear when communicating to my supervisees.

____ 3. My supervisees can trust me.

____ 4. I care about the welfare of my supervisees.

____ 5. I try hard to avoid failing in my job.

____ 6. It is important that I make it possible for my supervisees to find their work meaningful.

____ 7. I have the ability to identify the key issues in a situation.

____ 8. I am known to use unusual ways of getting my points across effectively.

____ 9. My supervisees can count on me to keep my commitments.

____10. I have a great deal of self-respect.

____11. I enjoy taking carefully calculated risks.

____12. I help my supervisees feel competent in what they do.

____13. I have a clear sense of priorities.

____14. I am in touch with how my supervisees feel.

____15. I rarely change my mind once I have taken a clear position.

____16. I focus on my supervisees' strengths.

____17. I feel most alive when I am deeply involved in a project.

____18. I let my supervisees know that we are all part of the same organizational community.

____19. I have a clear vision of the future of the organization.

____20. I communicate my feelings as well as my ideas.

____21. I let my supervisees know where I stand on important issues.

____22. I know how I fit into my organization.

____23. I believe that errors are not disasters but opportunities for learning.

____24. My supervisees enjoy being around me.

---

1 = Very Much Unlike Me; 2 = Somewhat Unlike Me;
3 = Neither Like or Unlike Me; 4 = Somewhat Like Me;
5 = Very Much Like Me

SCORING

The Management Style Survey is comprised of six scales. The items that appear on each scale are found below. To find your score, simply add together the numbers you used for the relevant items.

> Management of Attention Scale: 1, 7, 13, 19
> Management of Meaning Scale: 2, 8, 14, 20
> Management of Trust Scale: 3, 9, 15, 21
> Management of Self Scale: 4, 10, 16, 22
> Management of Risk Scale: 5, 11, 17, 23
> Management of Feelings Scale: 6, 12, 18, 24

NORMS

		SCORES				PERCENTILE
ATTN	MEAN	TRUST	SELF	RISK	FEEL	
19	17	20	17	18	17	85
17	16	18	15	16	15	70
15	14	16	13	14	13	50
13	12	14	11	12	11	30
11	11	12	9	10	9	15

High scores indicate greater levels of the relevant characteristic. If, for example, you received a percentile score of 85 on Attn, it means that 85 percent of people have less ability in Management of Attention than you do.

For more information see W. G. Bennis and B. Nanus, *The Strategies for Taking Charge* (New York: Harper & Row, 1985).

ABOUT THE MANAGEMENT STYLE SURVEY

Given the number of people I meet who tell me that Dilbert's pointy-haired manager captures their experience, it might be surprising to learn that there are, in fact, many highly effective managers. Organizational psychologists have been studying these people for more than half a century to understand what sets them apart from their pointy-haired colleagues, and we have learned a great deal. Unfortunately, much of this serious, scholarly, painstaking research is often overshadowed by the latest, momentary fad. One of the most widely respected of these scholars is Dr. Warren Bennis, who is well known for his theory of transformational leadership. He studied highly effective chief executive officers of major American corporations who were seen by their employees as successful, charismatic, and "inspired." Bennis concluded that these men and women possessed five basic behavior patterns—the first five scales on the test you just completed. These five characteristics elicited a specific set of emotional responses in their employees, and this factor is reflected in the sixth scale.

Management of Attention refers to a leader's ability to develop and communicate a clear vision for the future of his or her organization. As Bennis points out, it must be an attractive, realistic, and believable future. It is critical that this vision be developed in response to input from employees at all levels of the organization. The CEO who distributes a goal statement developed after consulting with only the top level of management will probably fail to inspire many people.

It should seem obvious, but if an organization is to be successful, it is critical that the managers and the workers have the same vision. I've risked stating the obvious because I have seen so many situations in which this is not the case. My wife has worked for a number of mortgage lenders where management's goal is to develop a reputation for integrity that will ensure their long-term success, but they have created an atmosphere in which loan officers are rewarded for their attempts to circumvent various rules and regulations for short-term gains. As another example, most college administrators seem to be concerned with increasing enrollment and reducing costs, while faculty are committed to educating students and conducting high-quality research. It always surprises me how often employees see their managers as "the enemy."

The second ability of effective managers, the Management of Meaning, refers to the leader's ability to communicate his or her message to mobilize employees, to help them adopt a new philosophy for their organizations. Effective managers are not afraid to use unusual or unorthodox methods to get their message across; their primary concern is that their message be understood.

Third, effective managers demonstrated Management of Trust. They were willing to follow through on promises, even if it became difficult to do so. They avoided "flip-flop" shifts in position; they were viewed as steady and dependable. Bennis reported that effective managers instilled trust by articulating a clear direction and sticking to it even during uncertain times.

This resulted in an organization that was permeated with a sense of integrity.

Management of Self, the fourth characteristic of effective managers, described the ability of effective leaders to utilize their strengths and their refusal to dwell on their weaknesses. They came across as confident to their employees, and this confidence was contagious. Managers who feel good about themselves and the role they play in the company are likely to have employees who also feel good about themselves and the role they play in the company.

The fifth quality, Management of Risk, reflected the observation that effective managers were not motivated by a CYA mentality. Yes, they carefully examined the odds of success or failure, but they were willing to take calculated risks and then invest a great deal of energy to ensure that their decisions paid off. As always, they inspired the same feeling in their employees, so no one in the organization felt it necessary to take a CYA approach to their jobs.

Bennis found that leaders who possessed the five qualities listed inspired an identifiable and consistent set of feelings in their employees. He labeled this phenomenon Management of Feelings. Employees who were fortunate enough to have such a leader felt that their work was important; they felt competent, and they experienced a sense of community with their colleagues. These employees had a strong sense of loyalty to their manager and their organization and enjoyed doing everything they could to help their organization reach its goals.

Researchers who study effective management techniques have had an ongoing debate about the extent to which leaders are born versus made. My answer to this question, bland as it may be, is "some of both." I believe that people who are self-confident and energetic and genuinely care about other people have much more potential to be effective managers than those without these qualities. On the other hand, I believe that almost anyone can become a more effective manager by studying what is known about management techniques and making a sustained effort to make any necessary changes. I do not believe, contrary to what some best-selling books suggest, that there are any worthwhile or productive shortcuts to becoming an effective manager.

If you received a low score on this test, it is possible for you to increase your managerial effectiveness. You can begin by focusing on those items that you responded to with less than a 5. You might endeavor, for instance, to pay closer attention to your supervisees when they are talking to you or to make a point of helping your employees feel competent about their work. There is also an abundance of excellent material about effective management and leadership. As well as looking at some of the popular books written for the general public, you might find it useful to read what scholarly researchers have learned about this topic—people like Warren Bennis, Bernard Bass, Peter Northhouse, and Karin Klenke.

It is extremely difficult to be as effective as the CEOs Bennis studied. But with a concerted effort you can avoid becoming just another pointy-haired manager.

PART IV

Being Prepared for the Right Job

After completing the tests in this section, you will know how skilled you are at finding the right job, and you will be able to match your personality characteristics with what your employer is looking for. These are the tests in Part IV:

CHAPTER 17

The Assertive Job Hunting Survey

This inventory is designed to provide information about the way in which you look for a job. Picture yourself in each of these job hunting situations and indicate how likely it is you would respond in the described manner. If you have never job hunted before, answer according to how you would like to try to find a job. Please respond to the following statements by using the key below.

1 = Very Unlikely
2 = Unlikely
3 = Somewhat Unlikely
4 = Somewhat Likely
5 = Likely
6 = Very Likely

---

* Reprinted with permission of Dr. Heather A. Becker.

_____1. When asked to indicate my experiences for a position, I would mention only my paid work experience.

_____2. If I heard someone talking about an interesting job opening, I'd be reluctant to ask for more information unless I knew the person.

_____3. I would ask an employer who did not have an opening if he knew of other employers who might have job openings.

_____4. I downplay my qualifications so that an employer won't think I'm more qualified than I am.

_____5. I would use an employment agency to find a job rather than apply to employers directly.

_____6. Before an interview, I would contact an employee of the organization to learn more about that organization.

_____7. I hesitate to ask questions when I'm being interviewed for a job.

_____8. I avoid contacting potential employers by phone or in person because I feel they are too busy to talk with me.

_____9. If an interviewer were very late for my interview, I would leave or arrange for another appointment.

_____10. I believe an experienced employment counselor would have a better idea of what jobs I should apply for than I would have.

_____11. If a secretary told me that a potential employer was too busy to see me, I would stop trying to contact that employer.

_____12. Getting the job I want is largely a matter of luck.

_____13. I'd directly contact the person for whom I would be working, rather than the personnel department of an organization.

_____14. I am reluctant to ask professors or supervisors to write letters of recommendation for me.

_____15. I would not apply for a job unless I had all the qualifications listed on the published job description.

_____16. I would ask an employer for a second interview if I felt the first one went poorly.

---

1 = Very Unlikely; 2 = Unlikely; 3 = Somewhat Unlikely;
4 = Somewhat Likely; 5 = Likely; 6 = Very Likely

_____17. I am reluctant to contact an organization about employment unless I know there is a job opening.

_____18. If I didn't get a job, I would call the employer and ask how I could improve my chances for a similar position.

_____19. I feel uncomfortable asking friends for job leads.

_____20. With the job market as tight as it is, I had better take whatever job I can get.

_____21. If the personnel office refused to refer me for an interview, I would directly contact the person I wanted to work for if I felt qualified for the position.

_____22. I would rather interview with recruiters who come to the college campus or job fairs than contact employers directly.

_____23. If an interviewer says, "I'll contact you if there are any openings," I figure there's nothing else I can do.

_____24. I'd check out available job openings before deciding what kind of job I'd like to have.

_____25. I am reluctant to contact someone I don't know for information about career fields in which I am interested.

1 = Very Unlikely; 2 = Unlikely; 3 = Somewhat Unlikely;
4 = Somewhat Likely; 5 = Likely; 6 = Very Likely

SCORING

Add your points for the following items: 3, 6, 9, 13, 16, 18, and 21. The remaining items are reverse scored. To obtain your points for these items, subtract the number you indicated from 7. Add the subsequent numbers together and find your total score by adding the totals for the two clusters of items. The reverse scored items are 1, 2, 4, 5, 7, 8, 10, 11, 12, 14, 15, 17, 19, 20, 22, 23, 24, and 25.

NORMS

SCORE	PERCENTILE
90	15
98	30
106	50
116	70
124	85

High scores indicate greater job hunting assertiveness. If, for example, you received a percentile score of 70, it means that 70 percent of people are lower in job hunting assertiveness than you are

For more information see H. A. Becker, "The Assertive Job-Hunting Survey," *Measurement and Evaluation in Guidance* 13 (1980): 43–48.

ABOUT THE ASSERTIVE JOB HUNTING SURVEY

Finding the right job requires both skill and effort. You are not likely to find the perfect ad waiting for you in the Sunday paper, since, as everyone knows, roughly 80 percent of job openings are not advertised. You have to know how to find those all-important leads, and you must have the necessary skills to take advantage of them once you do find them.

Dr. Heather Becker, the author of the Assertive Job Hunting Survey, developed this instrument to use in workshops at the Career Counseling Center at the University of Texas. The items on her scale reflect the kinds of problems that college seniors who were searching for that perfect job were especially likely to have. If you received a score lower than the 85th percentile, you could improve your odds of finding the job you want by improving your job hunting skills. Let us take a closer look at several of the items.

Consider items 1 and 4. Both of these items are relevant to the information you might have to fill out on an application form—incidentally, this would not be a good time to have an attack of modesty. List all your relevant experience, even if it was volunteer and even if it was somewhat tangential to the requirements of the position for which you are applying. In many cases, the application form is your first chance to make an impression on your future supervisor, and you want to do everything you can to ensure it is as favorable an impression as possible.

Another important reason to include all relevant experience and to emphasize your qualifications is that many companies are beginning to use biodata, the information on application forms. Personnel psychologists have learned that such information can be a powerful predictor of success on the job. In recent years, these psychologists have developed scoring systems that can be applied to biodata, and only those applicants with high scores are invited to proceed to the next step in the interview process. Because the use of biodata is relatively new, existing scoring systems are unique to specific companies, so it is not possible to provide you with definitive advice. It is a safe bet, however, that applicants who list several relevant volunteer positions and who indicate an impressive range of extracurricular activities will receive a higher biodata score than applicants who are fearful of appearing more qualified than they really are. Your goal at this point is to get the interview. You should not be worrying about creating unrealistically high expectations in your future boss.

Several of the items on Becker's survey reflect assertiveness about contacting companies and the people who know the most about open positions. Item five, for instance, asks about using an employment agency rather than contacting employers directly. Sure, it might be easier talking to someone who will earn a fee by helping you find a job than to someone who is harried from the task of selecting one employee from numerous applicants. But keep in mind that there is a good reason why companies are willing to hire an employment agency to help them find employees. Employers who pay these fees are usually the ones who cannot attract enough applicants on their own, and you may be eliminating the very best potential employers by relying on an employment agency.

Employers want enthusiastic, assertive employees. So browse through one of the available books about the best companies to work for. Contact the company directly. And rather than visiting the personnel office and letting it go at that, contact the person you would be working for. Personnel departments typically have a checklist of the requisite qualifications for the position, and if you do not match their specifications exactly, you could be out of luck. If you talk with the potential supervisor, you might be able to convince him or her that your background and skills are right for the job, even if you happen to be a year or two short on experience. Before you do this, though, be sure to do your homework about the company. Item 6 provides one useful suggestion for how to go about this.

One item that is especially near and dear to my heart is 14. I have known a number of students for whom I would have been happy to provide a very strong reference, but I was never asked to do so. I cannot believe that none of these students could have used an enthusiastic recommendation from a former professor.

On the other hand, I have been asked to write letters of reference for a number of students for whom it was difficult to think of anything to say that might be useful to them. I always tell such students the truth; for example, I might say that I do not know them very well, since they never said a word in class, and that I do not have a feel for their ability, since their grades in my course were mediocre. Curiously, I have never had a student say something like, "Thanks, I'll ask someone else who can write a stronger letter." Invariably these students tell me that they do not know anyone else they can ask. So they are willing to be damned by whatever faint praise I can provide.

The moral of the story is clear. Finding the right job is not something you can suddenly decide to do one day; it has to be an ongoing process. You do not want to have to settle for mediocre references. Build your resume as you go along. You want that manager of the fast food restaurant you worked at part time during high school to be happy to provide a reference for you later on. And you want to have at least three or four professors to remember you as one of those enthusiastic, capable students who make teaching a pleasure. Job hunting can be much easier when you have spent your life preparing for it.

CHAPTER 18
The Job Interview Self-statement Schedule

Imagine that you are being interviewed for a job and that you and the interviewer are the only persons present. The items in this questionnaire are intended to be like the thoughts you might have during a job interview. Apply the following two questions to each item and choose your answer from the relevant key.

* Reprinted with permission of Dr. Richard G. Heimberg.

a. *How Often*
   How often would this thought occur to you in a job interview?

   1 = Never
   2 = Seldom
   3 = Sometimes
   4 = Often
   5 = Constantly

b. *Help or Hinder*
   Should this thought occur to you, to what extent would it help or
   hinder your interview performance?

   1 = Not at All
   2 = A Little
   3 = Some
   4 = A Lot
   5 = A Great Deal

1. I am being humiliated.

    _____ a. How often?

    _____ b. Help or hinder?

2. I really have good qualifications for this job.

    _____ a. How often?

    _____ b. Help or hinder?

3. I'm usually better at things than most people, so I have a better chance of getting hired.

    _____ a. How often?

    _____ b. Help or hinder?

4. I can't think of a thing to say.

    _____ a. How often?

    _____ b. Help or hinder?

5. I feel like I dressed right for this interview.

    _____ a. How often?

    _____ b. Help or hinder?

6. When I leave, I will feel like I have done my best.

    _____ a. How often?

    _____ b. Help or hinder?

7. I would be very happy in this job.

    _____ a. How often?

    _____ b. Help or hinder?

8. I would be very good at this job.

    _____ a. How often?

    _____ b. Help or hinder?

---

a. 1 = Never; 2 = Seldom; 3 = Sometimes; 4 = Often; 5 = Constantly
b. 1 = Not at All; 2 = A Little; 3 = Some; 4 = A Lot; 5 = A Great Deal

9. I'm not expressing myself clearly.

_____ a. How often?

_____ b. Help or hinder?

10. I make a good impression on people.

_____ a. How often?

_____ b. Help or hinder?

11. I feel less qualified when I think about the other applicants.

_____ a. How often?

_____ b. Help or hinder?

12. I am feeling and coming across as confident.

_____ a. How often?

_____ b. Help or hinder?

13. I am afraid that I'll never be hired for anything.

_____ a. How often?

_____ b. Help or hinder?

14. I am really looking my best today.

_____ a. How often?

_____ b. Help or hinder?

15. I am not coming across as knowing enough about the position.

_____ a. How often?

_____ b. Help or hinder?

16. The interviewer has already made up his/her mind.

_____ a. How often?

_____ b. Help or hinder?

---

a. 1 = Never; 2 = Seldom; 3 = Sometimes; 4 = Often; 5 = Constantly
b. 1 = Not at All; 2 = A Little; 3 = Some; 4 = A Lot; 5 = A Great Deal

17. I am looking forward to meeting the people who work here.

____   a. How often?

____   b. Help or hinder?

18. This job would give me a good chance to get ahead.

____   a. How often?

____   b. Help or hinder?

19. The interviewer and I are on the same wavelength.

____   a. How often?

____   b. Help or hinder?

20. I wish I had more interview experience.

____   a. How often?

____   b. Help or hinder?

21. My voice is shaky.

____   a. How often?

____   b. Help or hinder?

22. The interviewer doesn't like "people like me."

____   a. How often?

____   b. Help or hinder?

23. I am saying all the wrong things.

____   a. How often?

____   b. Help or hinder?

24. This interview is not going well.

____   a. How often?

____   b. Help or hinder?

---

a. 1 = Never; 2 = Seldom; 3 = Sometimes; 4 = Often; 5 = Constantly
b. 1 = Not at All; 2 = A Little; 3 = Some; 4 = A Lot; 5 = A Great Deal

25. The interviewer is pleased with my qualifications.

_____ a. How often?

_____ b. Help or hinder?

26. I am freezing up under the pressure.

_____ a. How often?

_____ b. Help or hinder?

27. I am afraid that they will find out later than I'm not as competent as I have claimed.

_____ a. How often?

_____ b. Help or hinder?

28. I am expressing myself well.

_____ a. How often?

_____ b. Help or hinder?

29. I'm nervous and the interviewer knows it.

_____ a. How often?

_____ b. Help or hinder?

30. I'm doing a good job answering the interviewer's questions.

_____ a. How often?

_____ b. Help or hinder?

31. I will be myself, and that should be plenty.

_____ a. How often?

_____ b. Help or hinder?

32. This sounds interesting and exciting.

_____ a. How often?

_____ b. Help or hinder?

---

a. 1 = Never; 2 = Seldom; 3 = Sometimes; 4 = Often; 5 = Constantly
b. 1 = Not at All; 2 = A Little; 3 = Some; 4 = A Lot; 5 = A Great Deal

33. I expect the interviewer to like me.

____   a. How often?

____   b. Help or hinder?

34. I don't know what this person wants from me.

____   a. How often?

____   b. Help or hinder?

35. I really can do this job.

____   a. How often?

____   b. Help or hinder?

36. The more interviews I go on, the better I get.

____   a. How often?

____   b. Help or hinder?

37. I sound like I don't know what I am talking about.

____   a. How often?

____   b. Help or hinder?

38. I won't be able to say what I want before the interview ends.

____   a. How often?

____   b. Help or hinder?

39. The future looks promising.

____   a. How often?

____   b. Help or hinder?

40. I forgot the questions I was going to ask.

____   a. How often?

____   b. Help or hinder?

---

a. 1 = Never; 2 = Seldom; 3 = Sometimes; 4 = Often; 5 = Constantly
b. 1 = Not at All; 2 = A Little; 3 = Some; 4 = A Lot; 5 = A Great Deal

41. This place needs someone like me.

    ____ a. How often?

    ____ b. Help or hinder?

42. I won't be able to answer an important question.

    ____ a. How often?

    ____ b. Help or hinder?

43. I will cost myself this job by doing something stupid.

    ____ a. How often?

    ____ b. Help or hinder?

44. I am not qualified.

    ____ a. How often?

    ____ b. Help or hinder?

45. This is stressful.

    ____ a. How often?

    ____ b. Help or hinder?

46. I am not going to get this job.

    ____ a. How often?

    ____ b. Help or hinder?

47. This is what I want, and my attitude shows it.

    ____ a. How often?

    ____ b. Help or hinder?

---

a. 1 = Never; 2 = Seldom; 3 = Sometimes; 4 = Often; 5 = Constantly
b. 1 = Not at All; 2 = A Little; 3 = Some; 4 = A Lot; 5 = A Great Deal

48. I sound stupid.

    ____ a. How often?

    ____ b. Help or hinder?

49. This job is perfect for me, and I am perfect for this job.

    ____ a. How often?

    ____ b. Help or hinder?

50. I would feel terrific if I got this job.

    ____ a. How often?

    ____ b. Help or hinder?

a. 1 = Never; 2 = Seldom; 3 = Sometimes; 4 = Often; 5 = Constantly
b. 1 = Not at All; 2 = A Little; 3 = Some; 4 = A Lot; 5 = A Great Deal

SCORING

This test has two scales: the Negative Self-statement Scale and the Positive Self-statement Scale. For each of these scales, you can obtain two scores: one for assessing the frequency of self-statements (how often?) and one for assessing the impact of self-statements (help or hinder?). The first step in scoring this test is to find these four scores. The items reflecting positive and negative self-statements are listed below.

NEGATIVE SELF-STATEMENTS	POSITIVE SELF-STATEMENTS
1	2
4	3
9	5
11	6
13	7
15	8
16	10
20	12
21	14
22	17
23	18
24	19
26	25
27	28
29	30
34	31
37	32
38	33
40	35
42	36
43	39
44	41
45	47
46	49
48	50

To find your final score on the Negative Self-statement Scale, multiply the frequency score times the impact score. Repeat this procedure for the frequency and impact scores for the Positive Self-statement Items.

NORMS

POSITIVE	NEGATIVE	PERCENTILE
400	270	85
360	235	70
320	200	50
280	165	30
240	130	15

High scores indicate that you engage in more of the relevant self-statements. If, for example, you received a percentile score of 70 on Positive, it means that 70 percent of people utilize fewer positive self-statements than you do.

For more information see R. G. Heimberg, K. E. Keller, and T. Peca-Baker, "Cognitive Assessment of Social-Evaluative Anxiety in the Job Interview: Job Interview Self-statement Schedule," *Journal of Counseling Psychology* 33 (1986): 190–95.

ABOUT THE JOB INTERVIEW SELF-STATEMENT SCHEDULE

The employment interview is by far the procedure most widely used to select among applicants. Surveys have found that more than 95 percent of employers use the interview as an essential part of the selection process. Furthermore, employers may interview from five to twenty applicants for each available position. Needless to say, if you are to maximize your chances of getting that job, you must be prepared to perform your best during the interview. The Job Interview Self-statement Schedule, developed by Dr. Richard Heimberg, was intended to identify people whose anxiety and negative self-talk during the interview was likely to interfere with their ability to present their best side. If you scored higher than the 15th percentile on the Negative Self-statement Scale or if you failed to score at least at the 85th percentile on the Positive Self-statement Scale, you might benefit by working on the things you say to yourself during job interviews.

Before we talk about some specific ideas for changing your self-talk, let me offer a few reassuring words about employment interviews. First, researchers have found that interviewees begin the interview with a positive "halo." That is, the person interviewing you is likely to have a favorable impression about you before he or she meets you. This should not be surprising. After all, you had to present a convincing case that you were qualified for the job in order to receive the invitation for an interview. So, your task is relatively easy. You do not have to worry about making a good impression. All you have to do is maintain the halo you have already earned.

A second point to keep in mind is that employers often view the interview as an opportunity to "sell" the applicant on working for the company. This, of course, is especially likely to be true for jobs that are in high demand, such as for technical or information processing positions. So rather than focusing solely on your performance, you should keep in mind that the person interviewing you will probably be concerned with creating a favorable impression of the company.

Researchers have also learned that successful applicants are given longer interviews and that they tend to dominate the interview. So, to maximize your chances of receiving an offer at the end of the interview, you need to come across as a confident, assertive individual who is not afraid to ask questions. To do this, preparation is essential. Do your homework. Learn all you can about the company. Find out precisely what kind of person they are looking for and be prepared to offer them evidence that you fit the bill. Also, do not be reluctant to ask questions about issues that could influence your decision to accept a position. Although you want to be subtle about it, it never hurts to create the impression that your services are in demand and that you have several options open to you.

As the items on this test suggest, your thoughts during the interview process can influence the impression you make. If you have mostly self-critical thoughts, you may well freeze up and come across as nervous and lacking in confidence. On the other hand, if you can allow your positive thoughts to dominate, you are likely to appear relaxed, confident, and capable.

Psychologists have learned that thoughts are habits in much the same way as everyday behaviors are habits. Just as you might have a bad habit of biting your nails, you can have the bad habit of thinking about yourself in negative ways. The reality is that there is not always a connection between people's abilities and the way in which they think of themselves. We have all known, for example, people who had extremely high opinions of themselves despite their being intellectually limited jerks. On the other hand, we have all known capable, decent people who cannot think of a single positive thing to say about themselves. While we are likely to learn relatively soon after first meeting someone whether he or she is a self-aggrandizing dim-witted jerk, these people do make better first impressions than self-effacing, capable, and decent men and women. And job interviews rely on those critical first impressions.

If you find yourself preoccupied with negative thoughts during an interview (or, for that matter, any other time), force yourself to stop and substitute a more positive thought. For instance, if you find yourself thinking, "I sound like I don't know what I'm talking about," as item 37 suggests, force yourself to switch to a more positive thought, such as, "I'm doing a good job of

presenting my qualifications." Keep in mind that if you are the sort of person who allows negative thoughts to predominate, you are almost certainly a much harsher judge of yourself than others are. While you may think you sound as if you don't know what you are talking about, the chances are good the interviewer does not share your impression.

Also remember that even if your negative assessment of your performance is accurate, it can only serve to hinder your performance during the remainder of the interview. If you find yourself having negative thoughts, even if you suspect their accuracy, force yourself to switch to positive self-statements. If you can force yourself to think, "I am making a good impression," it will make it easier for you to present yourself as the capable, decent person you really are.

Making changes of any kind is never easy. You cannot expect to read these few words and go into your next interview with a completely new set of self-statements. If you are to change the way you think about yourself, you will have to practice—and practice hard. Begin with your family and your friends. Have them role-play job interviews with you. Extend your positive self-talk to your interactions with acquaintances and colleagues. As long as you persist, you will be successful in changing the way you evaluate yourself. And once you can be as positive about yourself as you deserve to be, you will be ready to knock the socks off the next person who offers you a job interview.

CHAPTER 19

The Cognitive Ability Test

There are three sections in the Cognitive Ability Test. Take as long as you like to complete each item and use scratch paper if necessary.

---

* Reprinted with permission of Dr. Louis H. Janda.

GENERAL INFORMATION

Select the best answer for each item.

1. What country is also a continent?

   a. United States

   b. Great Britain

   c. China

   d. Australia

2. What is "the windy city?"

   a. New York

   b. Detroit

   c. Chicago

   d. San Francisco

3. Who turned everything he touched into gold?

   a. Goldfinger

   b. Zeus

   c. King Midas

   d. Rapunzel

4. What is the length of a straight line that divides a circle into two equal parts called?

   a. the diameter

   b. the radius

   c. the tangent

   d. the secant

5. Which planet is known as the red planet?

   a. Mercury

   b. Venus

   c. Mars

   d. Jupiter

6. Who was president of the United States during the Civil War?

    a. George Washington

    b. Abraham Lincoln

    c. Andrew Jackson

    d. Thomas Jefferson

7. What is measured in fathoms?

    a. depth of water

    b. density of water

    c. temperature of water

    d. clarity of water

8. How many dimensions does a solid have?

    a. one

    b. two

    c. three

    d. four

9. What planet has the shortest year?

    a. Earth

    b. Pluto

    c. Mercury

    d. Uranus

10. Where is Mount Rushmore located?

    a. South Dakota

    b. Wyoming

    c. Montana

    d. Minnesota

11. What element do all organic compounds contain?

    a. nitrogen

    b. oxygen

    c. carbon

    d. ammonia

12. What is John Philip Sousa known for?

    a. sculpture

    b. music

    c. poetry

    d. paintings

13. How many miles are there in a kilometer?

    a. .4

    b. .6

    c. 1

    d. 1.6

14. Who wrote *Gone with the Wind*?

    a. Sylvia Plath

    b. Scarlet O'Hara

    c. Gertrude Stein

    d. Margaret Mitchell

15. Which U.S. state has the largest area?

    a. Texas

    b. Alaska

    c. California

    d. Montana

SYNONYMS

For each item, select the alternative that comes closest in meaning to the word in capital letters.

16. DILUTE
    a. exalt
    b. weaken
    c. purify
    d. dedicate

17. BOGUS
    a. replica
    b. simulation
    c. resemblance
    d. counterfeit

18. FORMULATE
    a. conceive
    b. multiply
    c. percolate
    d. perforate

19. DAWDLE
    a. loiter
    b. draw
    c. crawl
    d. writhe

20. CONTENT
    a. shape
    b. hinder
    c. satisfied
    d. appalled

21. REVEAL
    a. divulge
    b. betray
    c. reify
    d. rejoice

22. CABINET
    a. bureau
    b. federal
    c. open
    d. drawer

23. HOBNOB
    a. nail
    b. saddle
    c. encumber
    d. socialize

24. OSTENTATIOUS
    a. generous
    b. brilliance
    c. pecuniary
    d. pretentious

25. PEAK
    a. look
    b. glimpse
    c. summit
    d. tear

26. PROMINENT

    a. conspicuous

    b. tawdry

    c. brazen

    d. shameless

27. ABDICATE

    a. appease

    b. suggest

    c. dictate

    d. resign

28. MORALE

    a. goodness

    b. mood

    c. virtue

    d. purity

29. LEVY

    a. song

    b. carry

    c. convey

    d. assessment

30. WRETCH

    a. tool

    b. wicked

    c. ugly

    d. fiend

ARITHMETIC

For each item, select the correct answer. Use scratch paper if necessary.

31. The average daily low temperature in Canada during January is -15°. If the average daily low temperature in Florida is 62° higher, what would that temperature be?

    a. -77°

    b. 42°

    c. 47°

    d. 77°

32. $26 \div 8 = ?$

    a. 3.00

    b. 3.15

    c. 3.2

    d. 3.25

33. Susan has 70 percent as much money as Twana. If Twana has $58.00, how much does Susan have?

    a. $38.40

    b. $40.60

    c. $41.60

    d. $46.00

34. $2/3 \times 1.5 = ?$

    a. $3/4$

    b. $4/6$

    c. 1

    d. 1.5

35. $2^2 \div 2^3 = ?$

    a. .25

    b. .5

    c. .67

    d. 2

36. $3/2 \div 2/3 = ?$

    a. .40

    b. .50

    c. 2.00

    d. 2.25

37. It took Miko $4 1/2$ hours to travel 180 miles. How fast was she driving?

    a. 40 mph

    b. 45 mph

    c. 48 mph

    d. 52 mph

38. $1/4 \times 2/3 \times 3/2 = ?$

    a. 1/4

    b. $5/9$

    c. $6/9$

    d. 3

39. $1/4 \times 3/4 \div 4/5 = ?$

    a. $7/13$

    b. $15/64$

    c. $15/40$

    d. $12/20$

40. Of the 60 people in the club, 36 are men. What percentage of the members are women?

    a. 20 percent

    b. 24 percent

    c. 40 percent

    d. 48 percent

41. A shirt cost $20.80 after a 35 percent discount. What was the original price?

    a. $28.00

    b. $32.00

    c. $36.00

    d. $41.60

42. One side of a rectangle is 3 feet, and the diagonal is 5 feet. What is the area?

    a. 6 feet

    b. 7.5 feet

    c. 12 feet

    d. 15 feet

43. The hypotenuse of a right triangle is 5 feet, and its area is 6 square feet. How many feet is one of the sides of the triangle?

    a. 1.2 feet

    b. 2 feet

    c. 2.5 feet

    d. 4 feet

44. Todd scored 80 percent as many points in a basketball game as Jeremy did. If Todd scored 20 points, how many points did Jeremy score?

    a. 16

    b. 24

    c. 25

    d. 26

45. The diagonal of a rectangle is 5 feet, and one side is four feet. What is the perimeter?

    a. 12 feet

    b. 14 feet

    c. 16 feet

    d. 18 feet

SCORING

The following are the correct answers. Add your correct responses together to find your score.

1.	d	16.	b	31.	c
2.	c	17.	d	32.	d
3.	c	18.	a	33.	b
4.	a	19.	a	34.	c
5.	c	20.	c	35.	b
6.	b	21.	a	36.	d
7.	a	22.	a	37.	a
8.	c	23.	d	38.	a
9.	c	24.	d	39.	b
10.	a	25.	c	40.	c
11.	c	26.	a	41.	b
12.	b	27.	d	42.	c
13.	b	28.	b	43.	d
14.	d	29.	d	44.	c
15.	b	30.	d	45.	b

NORMS

SCORE	PERCENTILE
32	85
28	70
24	50
20	30
16	15

High scores indicate greater cognitive ability. If, for instance, you received a percentile score of 70, it means that 70 percent of people have lower cognitive ability than you do.

For more information see L. H. Janda, *Psychological Testing: Theory and Applications* (Boston: Allyn and Bacon, 1998). The author wishes to thank Lek Wanichtanom for her help in developing this test.

ABOUT THE COGNITIVE ABILITY TEST

Over the past decade or two there has been a dramatic shift in the way in which personnel psychologists view tests of cognitive ability. As recently as the 1970s, the conventional wisdom was that job requirements were very specific. That is, a test that proved to be useful to select successful employees in one setting would probably not be useful in a different, albeit similar, setting. The belief was that every job had unique elements and that to be useful, selection tests had to reflect these specific elements.

In the late 1970s, Drs. Frank Schmidt and Jack Hunter, both research personnel psychologists, began to build a compelling case that this view was based on faulty research methods. Their arguments and the evidence they gathered to back them up were so compelling that currently a substantial majority of personnel psychologists agree that tests of cognitive ability are the best tools that employers have available to them to predict success on the job. By the way, the term *cognitive ability* is synonymous with *intelligence*, but for reasons I do not understand, personnel psychologists prefer the former term.

The work of Schmidt and Hunter resulted in a concept called validity generalization. This view suggests that a test of cognitive ability will be valid for all jobs in the same broad category and across all settings. The concept of validity generalization has profound implications. It suggests, for instance, that the same test

that can effectively select the best automobile mechanics can also be used to select the best secretaries, the best computer programmers, the best managers, the best electricians—the best from virtually any job category. This suggests that it is pointless to utilize complex aptitude batteries, so popular until the 1970s, that measure a variety of specific skills. Schmidt and Hunter argue that a single test of general cognitive ability will do as well in selecting successful employees for any particular job as will a test designed to measure the skills specific to that job.

Schmidt and Hunter do not deny that jobs demand distinct patterns of specific skills; they simply argue that these patterns are irrelevant to selecting successful employees. To explain this, they developed an investment theory of ability. This theory suggests that people with specific interests will "invest" their general cognitive ability in developing associated skills and are likely to pursue jobs that reflect both their interests and their skills. It is likely, therefore, that anyone who is applying for a position as, say, an electrician, will have spent considerable time learning about such things. As a group, electricians are likely to have considerably more electrical knowledge than a group of people who have had a lifelong interest in, say, literature, and vice versa. However, a test of general cognitive ability is related to how much knowledge persons have acquired in general and how well they can apply this knowledge in response to the novel demands of their jobs.

If you received a high score on this test, you have a distinct advantage. You probably find it relatively painless to acquire the knowledge and skills you need for your career, and you will perform well enough on selection tests to make you an attractive applicant to a variety of employers. A high score, however, is far from a guarantee of success. Yes, you have an edge over your less intelligent peers, but unless you are willing to develop and utilize the other qualities discussed in this book, you will lose your advantage in short order. Being bright does not give you a free pass.

If you were disappointed with your score, you should not use this as an excuse to become discouraged and give up. As effective as tests of cognitive ability are at predicting job success, they are far from perfect. And employers know that. You can compete successfully with your more intelligent peers if you develop your skills, acquire relevant experience, and strive to become the sort of person who will be thought of as a valued colleague.

It is also the case that you can improve your ability to perform well on tests such as this one by studying and practicing. To some degree, intelligence does reflect a biological capacity, but it is impossible to measure a person's innate ability. All we psychologists can do is estimate intelligence by measuring the effects of education. Bright people acquire better vocabularies, they develop the ability to solve math problems quickly, they absorb a wider range of information from reading the newspaper, and consequently, they answer more items correctly on tests of cognitive ability. So, you can compensate for a low score by making an extra effort to acquire the knowledge and skills you need to perform well on such tests. Make a concerted effort to improve your vocabulary. Rather than watch reruns of *The Simpsons* every evening, spend an hour reading news magazines. Study guides that students use to prepare for the SAT can be especially helpful if you need to hone your math skills. Such a self-improvement program will help you not only to do well on a test of cognitive ability the next time a potential employers asks you to take one but also to achieve the career success you want and deserve.

CHAPTER 20

The Integrity Test

The following statements reflect behaviors and attitudes related to honesty in the workplace. Use the guidelines below to indicate the degree to which each statement describes your behavior or attitudes.

5 = Very Accurate
4 = Accurate
3 = Neither Accurate nor Inaccurate
2 = Inaccurate
1 = Very Inaccurate

____ 1. I have stolen money from my employer.

____ 2. I have stolen merchandise from my employer.

____ 3. I have taken office supplies home for my personal use.

____ 4. I have overcharged customers and kept the money for myself.

____ 5. I have looked the other way when friends or coworkers have stolen from my employer.

____ 6. I have given my friends merchandise without asking for payment.

____ 7. I have falsified company records or reports.

____ 8. I have used company resources (e.g., long distance phone calls, gas credit cards) for unauthorized purposes.

____ 9. I have used my employee discount to make purchases for friends.

____ 10. I have sold merchandise to my friends and kept the money for myself.

____ 11. I have made a habit of arriving at work late.

____ 12. I miss work without a legitimate reason.

____ 13. I have faked illness to avoid going to work.

____ 14. I have stolen things from coworkers.

____ 15. I have gone to work intoxicated or high.

____ 16. I have damaged company equipment or merchandise intentionally.

____ 17. I try to do as little work as possible.

____ 18. I have faked an injury in an attempt to receive workman's compensation.

____ 19. I have worked in a slow and sloppy fashion intentionally.

____ 20. I have left work early without permission.

____ 21. Most people steal at least small things from their employers.

____ 22. Most people, if they could be assured they would not be caught, would steal money from their employers.

---

5 = Very Accurate; 4 = Accurate; 3 = Neither Accurate nor Inaccurate;
2 = Inaccurate; 1 = Very Inaccurate

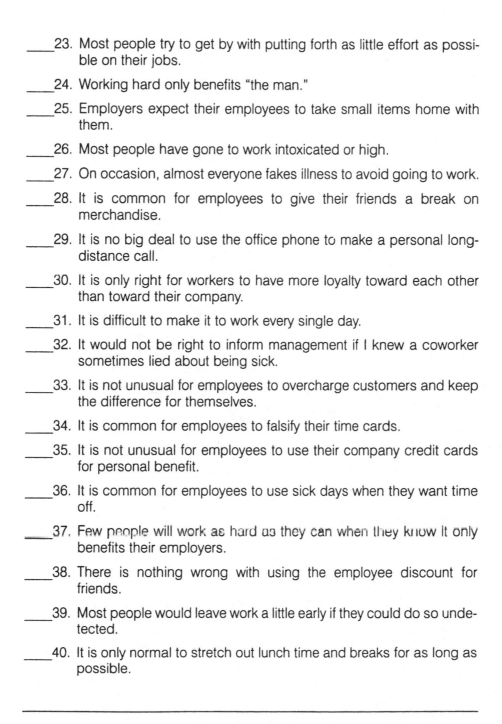

____23. Most people try to get by with putting forth as little effort as possible on their jobs.

____24. Working hard only benefits "the man."

____25. Employers expect their employees to take small items home with them.

____26. Most people have gone to work intoxicated or high.

____27. On occasion, almost everyone fakes illness to avoid going to work.

____28. It is common for employees to give their friends a break on merchandise.

____29. It is no big deal to use the office phone to make a personal long-distance call.

____30. It is only right for workers to have more loyalty toward each other than toward their company.

____31. It is difficult to make it to work every single day.

____32. It would not be right to inform management if I knew a coworker sometimes lied about being sick.

____33. It is not unusual for employees to overcharge customers and keep the difference for themselves.

____34. It is common for employees to falsify their time cards.

____35. It is not unusual for employees to use their company credit cards for personal benefit.

____36. It is common for employees to use sick days when they want time off.

____37. Few people will work as hard as they can when they know It only benefits their employers.

____38. There is nothing wrong with using the employee discount for friends.

____39. Most people would leave work a little early if they could do so undetected.

____40. It is only normal to stretch out lunch time and breaks for as long as possible.

5 = Very Accurate; 4 = Accurate; 3 = Neither Accurate nor Inaccurate;
2 = Inaccurate; 1 = Very Inaccurate

SCORING

To obtain your score, simply add together the values of your responses.

NORMS

SCORE	PERCENTILE
86	85
82	70
78	50
72	30
68	15

High scores indicate greater dishonesty. If, for instance, you received a percentile score of 70, it means that 70 percent of people are more honest than you are.

For more information see John W. Jones, *Preemployment Honesty Testing* (New York: Quorum Books, 1991).

ABOUT THE INTEGRITY TEST

Integrity tests are a relatively recent phenomenon. Until 1988, when President Reagan signed into law the Employee Polygraph Protection Act, many employers used the polygraph, commonly called the lie detector, to identify potentially dishonest employees. But business loses as much as $40 billion each year from employee dishonesty, so employers were not about to give up in their attempt to weed out dishonest workers. Once the use of the polygraph was made illegal, the integrity test industry rushed in to fill the void.

Integrity tests fall into two broad categories. The first is called personality-based integrity tests (the Conscientiousness Scale, presented in chapter 25, is an example of this type). The second category includes overt integrity tests (the test you just completed is an example of this variety). Overt integrity tests typically include two types of items. The first type, represented by the first twenty items on this integrity test, encourages examinees to make overt admissions of theft and other illegal or undesirable activities including substance abuse and poor work habits. Paradoxical as it may be, dishonest people are apparently honest enough to admit their dishonesty—at least some of it.

The second type of item measures attitudes or beliefs about the extent of employee theft and various undesirable work behaviors. Dishonest people tend to have more cynical attitudes about such behaviors and believe they are more common than do honest people. And indeed, it does make sense that people who regularly take merchandise home or call in sick so that they can have a day off would justify their behavior by asserting that "everyone does it."

The integrity test you just completed is not one that is actually used by business. Such tests are copyrighted by their developers; to protect their products, the companies that publish them do not release either the scoring keys or the norms to anyone. Employers are provided with only a "recommend" or "don't recommend" result. Consequently, it is impossible to say for certain which category your score would yield. Given the reports that about half of all those who take such tests are identified as being potentially dishonest, it does seem safe to conclude that a score below the 50th percentile would yield a "recommend" report.

Integrity tests, especially overt integrity tests, are extremely controversial. On the one hand, there is clear evidence that such tests do what they are intended to do—identify potentially dishonest employees. But, on the other hand, integrity tests are like all other psychological tests in that they are far from perfect in the predictions they yield. The U.S. Office of Technology has estimated that over 90 percent of those who fail such tests (about one million people each year) are incorrectly labeled as dishonest. It should not be surprising that so many people object to such tests, when there is such a large number of errors—especially when an incorrect label can be so damaging.

A common objection to integrity tests is that they represent an invasion of privacy—the same objection, by the way, that led to the banning of the use of the polygraph in pre-employment screening. This view has led Massachusetts to ban the use of overt integrity tests by employers, and several other states have similar legislation pending. Personnel psychologists defend the use of such tests by asserting that because honesty is clearly related to job performance, employers have a right to ask potential employees if they have been dishonest in their previous positions. A company that has honest employees will certainly be more successful than one that employs thieves.

But the issue at hand is what should you do when faced with a test such as the one here. As is obvious, low scores on the integrity test are good; they suggest employees who will be honest and who will perform their jobs in a diligent fashion. So, clearly, it would be good for you to receive a low score on this test.

Keep in mind, though, that the specific test you take may include a subscale to detect lying (i.e., a lie scale to determine if you are being honest on the integrity test—the irony of which is too complex for my mind to grasp). So my strong belief that one should never try to be deceptive when taking any psychological test applies here as well. It rarely pays off, and it is likely to be self-defeating in the long run. But it is important to respond to the items with the proper frame of mind. If I were to take the test while in a cynical and self-flagellating mood, I might not come off looking too good. A pen or two has found its way from my office to my house,

in my younger days I had jobs in which I "paced" myself so that I would be fresh for the evening's activities, and I remember giving friends free food on occasion, when I worked at a fast-food restaurant. So, if I were to be brutally honest, I might appear to have my share of moral lacunae (again, this is thick with irony). But if I were feeling good about myself and responded to the items in a way that reflected my behavior 99.9 percent of the time, I feel confident the test results would yield a recommendation that I be hired.

If you are interested enough in your career to be reading this book, I would be surprised if you were to have any difficulty with an integrity test. If you were not a reasonably bright, hard-working, conscientious person, you would not spend your time trying to increase the odds of finding the career best suited for you. So my best advice is for you to respond to the items truthfully, but not brutally so. Present yourself as you are at least 99 percent of the time and don't obsess about a few youthful indiscretions. If you are an honest person, tests of this type will not present much of a problem for you.

One final thought. Many publishers of integrity tests have found that their instruments work best if they deceive the people taking them (does the irony ever end?). So tests of this type may be presented as tests of "General Personality Characteristics," or "General Attitudes Toward the Workplace." Be assured, however, that if the test includes items requesting admissions to theft or about attitudes toward theft, it is, in fact, an integrity test.

CHAPTER 21

The Neuroticism Scale

The following phrases describe people's behaviors. Use the rating scale below to describe how accurately each statement describes you. Describe yourself as you generally are now, not as you wish to be in the future. Describe yourself as you honestly see yourself in relation to other people you know who are of the same sex and age as you are.

1 = Very Inaccurate
2 = Moderately Inaccurate
3 = Neither Inaccurate nor Accurate
4 = Moderately Accurate
5 = Very Accurate

* Adapted from Dr. Lewis Goldberg of the Oregon Research Institute.

_____ 1. I worry about things.

_____ 2. I rarely complain.

_____ 3. I am very pleased with myself.

_____ 4. I am easily intimidated.

_____ 5. I never splurge.

_____ 6. I panic easily.

_____ 7. I adapt easily to new situations.

_____ 8. I get angry easily.

_____ 9. I often feel blue.

_____10. I am able to stand up for myself.

_____11. I often eat too much.

_____12. I am calm even in tense situations.

_____13. I don't worry about things that have already happened.

_____14. I get irritated easily.

_____15. I dislike myself.

_____16. I am not bothered by difficult social situations.

_____17. I never spend more than I can afford.

_____18. I become overwhelmed by events.

_____19. I fear for the worst.

_____20. I get upset easily.

_____21. I feel comfortable with myself.

_____22. I am afraid that I will do the wrong thing.

_____23. I am able to control my cravings.

_____24. I readily overcome setbacks.

---

1 = Very Inaccurate; 2 = Moderately Inaccurate;
3 = Neither Inaccurate nor Accurate; 4 = Moderately Accurate;
5 = Very Accurate

____25. I am afraid of many things.

____26. I keep my cool.

____27. I am often down in the dumps.

____28. I find it difficult to approach others.

____29. I don't know why I do some of the things I do.

____30. I know how to cope.

____31. I am not easily disturbed by events.

____32. I am often in a bad mood.

____33. I have a low opinion of myself.

____34. I am afraid to draw attention to myself.

____35. I do things I later regret.

____36. I can handle complex problems.

____37. I get stressed out easily.

____38. I am not easily annoyed.

____39. I have frequent mood swings.

____40. I am comfortable in unfamiliar situations.

____41. I easily resist temptations.

____42. I remain calm under pressure.

____43. I get caught up in my problems.

____44. I seldom get mad.

____45. I seldom feel blue.

____46. I only feel comfortable with friends.

____47. I rarely overindulge.

____48. I feel that I'm unable to deal with things.

1 = Very Inaccurate; 2 = Moderately Inaccurate;
3 = Neither Inaccurate nor Accurate; 4 = Moderately Accurate;
5 = Very Accurate

____49. I am not easily bothered by things.

____50. I rarely get irritated.

____51. I feel that my life lacks direction.

____52. I stumble over my words.

____53. I go on binges.

____54. I can't make up my mind.

____55. I am relaxed most of the time.

____56. I lose my temper.

____57. I feel desperate.

____58. I am not embarrassed easily.

____59. I love to eat.

____60. I get overwhelmed by emotions.

1 = Very Inaccurate; 2 = Moderately Inaccurate;
3 = Neither Inaccurate nor Accurate; 4 = Moderately Accurate;
5 = Very Accurate

SCORING

The Neuroticism Scale is comprised of six subscales. The items appearing on each subscale appear below. Items marked with an asterisk (*) are reverse scored.

Anxiety (Ax):	1, 7*, 13*, 19, 25, 31*, 37, 43, 49*, 55*
Anger (Ar):	2*, 8, 14, 20, 26*, 32, 38*, 44*, 50*, 56
Depression (De):	3*, 9, 15, 21*, 27, 33, 39, 45*, 51, 57
Self-Consciousness (Sc):	4, 10*, 16*, 22, 28, 34, 40*, 46, 52, 58*
Immoderation (Im):	5*, 11, 17*, 23*, 29, 35, 41*, 47*, 53, 59
Vulnerability (Vu):	6, 12*, 18, 24*, 30*, 36*, 42*, 48, 54, 60

NORMS

Ax	Ar	De	Sc	Im	Vu	Total	Percentile
32	30	29	33	34	27	186	85
27	25	24	28	29	22	154	70
21	19	18	22	23	17	121	50
15	13	13	16	17	12	88	30
10	10	10	11	12	10	60	15

For more information see L. R. Goldberg, "An Alternative 'Description of Personality': The Big-Five Factor Structure," *Journal of Personality and Social Psychology* 59 (1990): 1216–29.

ABOUT THE NEUROTICISM SCALE

For the past ten years or so, one of the hottest areas of psychological research has been with the "Big Five." The Big Five is so named because it is believed that the five areas represented are the five basic dimensions of personality. In other words, the five traits that comprise the Big Five can account for most of the almost infinite variety in the personalities of men and women. The Big Five includes the test you just completed, a measure of Neuroticism, as well as the traits measured by the tests in the following four sections: Agreeableness, Extroversion, Openness, and Conscientiousness.

The Big Five has been the focus of research of psychologists with a variety of specialties, but it has been of particular interest to personnel psychologists. Since hundreds of tests have been found to be related to job success, the idea that a single test measuring only five dimensions might predict success in a variety of occupations has a great deal of appeal. Obviously, it would be much more efficient to administer applicants a single test, regardless of the specific position they were applying for, than to select the best two or three tests from among several hundred. Work in this area is too new for us to be able to conclude that our tests of the Big Five will make all others obsolete, but there has been enough research to conclude that scores on these tests are good predictors of job success across a variety of occupations.

The specific tests of the Big Five presented here were developed by Dr. Lewis Goldberg of the University of Oregon. His tests provide essentially the same information as does the most widely used commercial test of the Big Five, the NEO Personality Inventory. Because the NEO, as well as other similar tests, can be quite expensive to use, Goldberg believed that research regarding the Big Five was unnecessarily impeded by the cost of testing materials. Goldberg provided his tests free to anyone who might want to use them, so researchers who are interested in expanding their knowledge in this area do not have to concern themselves with their tight academic budgets. Goldberg's contribution has been invaluable, and all of us who do work in this area owe him a debt of gratitude.

Each one of the Big Five dimensions consists of six subscales, usually called facets. As you can see from scoring this test, Neuroticism consists of Anxiety, Anger, Depression, Self-consciousness, Immoderation, and Vulnerability. The meaning of scores on the first three facets is straightforward. High scores mean that you are above average in your levels of anxiety, anger, and depression. Anger, by the way, is one characteristic employers are especially interested in. Angry employees have the potential to cause all manner of problems, ranging from destruction of property to contributing to friction among employees.

Self-consciousness has been called social anxiety by some theorists. High scorers on this scale tend to be unassertive in social situations, especially around people they do not know well, and they are likely to be easily intimidated.

People who score high on the Immoderation facet tend to have poor impulse control. They are also more likely than low scorers to have problems with alcohol or drug abuse.

People who score high on the Vulnerability facet are those who are likely to become flustered and find it difficult to perform their jobs under stressful circumstances. In other words, they seem to be especially vulnerable to difficult circumstances. Clearly, you are fortunate if you received scores below the 50th percentile on all of these facets.

There are dozens of published studies that have found that neuroticism scores are related to job success (negatively related, of course) in a variety of occupations. Let me provide you with just a few examples. Dr. Michael Eysenck and his colleagues at the University of London found that academic staff who score high on neuroticism were poor at structuring their work, did not like challenging work, and did not believe there was a connection between ability and performance. Eastern Washington University psychologists Drs. Cass and James Dykeman found that successful nationally certified executive search recruiters received lower than average scores on a measure of neuroticism. Dr. Edward Walker and his colleagues at the University of Washington found that neurotic physicians were especially likely to become frustrated when caring for patients suffering with rheumatological complaints. And finally, Dr. Daniel Steel and his colleagues from Lincoln University of New Zealand reported that among Antarctic personnel, Italians were less neurotic than personnel of other nationalities. As interesting as this finding may be, one wonders how many employers will find this type of information useful.

Employers do, however, find the Neuroticism Scale useful. There is evidence, for example, that it can predict disruptive behaviors at work. Neurotic employees are more likely to abuse alcohol, they have more conflicts with their colleagues, and they are more likely to make disability claims than their emotionally stable colleagues. If you received high scores on one or more of the facets, you may benefit from taking steps to increase your emotional stability. There are a number of good self-help books that can get you started in the right direction, and you may also find it useful to seek professional help. Neuroticism can interfere not only with your ability to have a successful career but also with your ability to have a happy and satisfying life. Do not settle for less than you have to.

CHAPTER 22

The Agreeableness Scale

The following phrases describe people's behaviors. Use the rating scale below to describe how accurately each statement describes you. Describe yourself as you generally are now, not as you wish to be in the future. Describe yourself as you honestly see yourself in relation to other people you know who are of the same sex and age as you are.

1 = Very Inaccurate
2 = Moderately Inaccurate
3 = Neither Inaccurate nor Accurate
4 = Moderately Accurate
5 = Very Accurate

---

* Adapted from Dr. Lewis Goldberg of the Oregon Research Institute.

_____ 1. I trust others.

_____ 2. I obstruct others' plans.

_____ 3. I make people feel welcome.

_____ 4. I am easy to satisfy.

_____ 5. I make myself the center of attention.

_____ 6. I can't stand weak people.

_____ 7. I believe that people are essentially evil.

_____ 8. I would never cheat on my taxes.

_____ 9. I take no time for others.

_____10. I can't stand confrontations.

_____11. I dislike being the center of attention.

_____12. I sympathize with the homeless.

_____13. I am wary of others.

_____14. I stick to the rules.

_____15. I anticipate the needs of others.

_____16. I hate to seem pushy.

_____17. I dislike talking about myself.

_____18. I feel sympathy for those who are worse off than myself.

_____19. I suspect hidden motives in others.

_____20. I take advantage of others.

_____21. I love to help others.

_____22. I have a sharp tongue.

_____23. I boast about my virtues.

_____24. I value cooperation over competition.

---

1 = Very Inaccurate; 2 = Moderately Inaccurate;
3 = Neither Inaccurate nor Accurate; 4 = Moderately Accurate;
5 = Very Accurate

____25. I believe that others have good intentions.

____26. I use flattery to get ahead.

____27. I am concerned about others.

____28. I contradict others.

____29. I consider myself an average person.

____30. I suffer from others' sorrows.

____31. I trust what people say.

____32. I use others for my own ends.

____33. I have a good word for everyone.

____34. I love a good fight.

____35. I seldom toot my own horn.

____36. I am not interested in other people's problems.

____37. I believe that people are basically moral.

____38. I know how to get around the rules.

____39. I look down on others.

____40. I yell at people.

____41. I believe that I am better than others.

____42. I tend to dislike soft-hearted people.

____43. I believe in human goodness.

____44. I cheat to get ahead.

____45. I am indifferent to the feelings of others.

____46. I insult people.

____47. I think highly of myself.

____48. I believe in an eye for an eye.

---

1 = Very Inaccurate; 2 = Moderately Inaccurate;
3 = Neither Inaccurate nor Accurate; 4 = Moderately Accurate;
5 = Very Accurate

____49. I think that all will be well.

____50. I put people under pressure.

____51. I make people feel uncomfortable.

____52. I get back at others.

____53. I have a high opinion of myself.

____54. I try not to think about the needy.

____55. I distrust people.

____56. I pretend to be concerned for others.

____57. I turn my back on others.

____58. I hold a grudge.

____59. I know the answers to many questions.

____60. I believe people should fend for themselves.

1 = Very Inaccurate; 2 = Moderately Inaccurate;
3 = Neither Inaccurate nor Accurate; 4 = Moderately Accurate;
5 = Very Accurate

SCORING

The Agreeableness Scale is comprised of six subscales. The items appearing on each subscale appear below. Items marked with an asterisk (*) are reverse scored.

Trust (Tr): 1, 7*, 13*, 19*, 25, 31, 37, 43, 49, 55*
Morality (Mr): 2*, 8, 14, 20*, 26*, 32*, 38*, 44*, 50*, 56*
Altruism (Al): 3, 9*, 15, 21, 27, 33, 39*, 45*, 51*, 57*
Cooperation (Co): 4, 10, 16, 22*, 28*, 34*, 40*, 46*, 52*, 58*
Modesty (Md): 5*, 11, 17, 23*, 29, 35, 41*, 47*, 53*, 59*
Sympathy (Sy): 6*, 12, 18, 24, 30, 36*, 42*, 48*, 54*, 60*

NORMS

TR	MR	AL	CO	MD	SY	TOTAL	PERCENTILE
43	42	45	43	37	40	250	85
38	38	41	38	32	35	221	70
33	33	36	33	26	30	191	50
28	28	31	28	20	25	161	30
23	24	27	23	15	20	132	15

For more information see L. R. Goldberg, "An Alternative 'Description of Personality': The Big-Five Factor Structure," *Journal of Personality and Social Psychology* 59 (1990): 1216–29.

ABOUT THE AGREEABLENESS SCALE

Agreeableness is the second dimension of the Big Five. While not as powerful a predictor as Neuroticism or, as we shall see shortly, Conscientiousness, Agreeableness has been found to be related to performance in a variety of occupations. Interestingly, though, sometimes this relationship is positive, and sometimes, in other situations, the relationship between test scores and job proficiency is negative. This means that it is not possible to come to the general conclusion that high scores are better than low scores. There are some jobs for which low scores predict success.

Before we provide examples, let us take a minute to review the six facets of Agreeableness. Trust is self-evident. People who score high on this dimension tend to believe the best about people. They assume that most people are honest, decent, and trustworthy, and they will continue to hold these beliefs unless they are presented with compelling evidence to the contrary. Low scorers assume that people cannot be counted on to say what they mean and that one should always be concerned with possible hidden motives a colleague might harbor.

Those who score high on the Morality facet have a strong sense of right and wrong. They live by the rules and pride themselves on treating other people fairly. Low scorers are more cynical and manipulative. They evaluate relationships in terms of what they can get from them and believe that rules are meant to be bent, if not broken.

Altruism refers to the desire to help other people and to do nice things for them purely for the pleasure of doing so. High scorers feel good when they make other people feel good. Low scorers, on the other hand, can be nice, but only when they have an ulterior motive. For them, helping others is a waste of time, unless they can expect to get something in return.

High scorers on the Cooperation facet want to avoid being seen as promoting themselves. They live by the cliché that the best way to get along is to go along. They tend to be forgiving people and at times carry this to the point where others view them as doormats. Low scorers are competitive people. They believe that to get to the top, one must step on a number of backs. They do not avoid confrontations. Indeed, they usually enjoy them, since they provide the opportunity to demonstrate superiority.

Modest people have modest self-esteem. They do not think of themselves as having any particular skills or expertise, and even if they did, they would be reluctant to let others know about it. Their immodest colleagues, on the other hand, love to let the world know what wonderful, competent people they are. They are not limited by a need to be accurate when talking about their skills and knowledge.

Like Bill Clinton, those high on the Sympathy facet can feel your pain. They are concerned with people less fortunate than themselves and are likely to translate this concern into action. Low scorers rarely think about the "less fortunate," but when they do, they are likely to conclude that their lowly status reflects their weakness and shortcomings.

People with high scores on the Agreeableness Scale do well in service-type jobs. They make excellent social workers, clergy, and psychologists. They are likely to do well in the types of jobs, such as in customer service, that demand the ability to interact effectively with the public. These people usually make valued office workers because they place such a high value on getting along. They are quick to offer their colleagues help when they need it, they are concerned with doing their fair share of work, and they have no need to prove themselves better than anyone else.

One's score on the Agreeableness Scale also predicts success in training programs. Companies that require extensive training before employees are actually placed on the job may look for agreeable people.

Agreeableness is negatively related to desire for achievement, so high scorers are not always the most successful people. The company who wants to hire a manager to turn a department around would want to find someone with at least a moderately low score on this dimension. Turning things around may mean terminating some employees or making reassignments that are almost certain to inconvenience some people. Successful managers are not bothered (at least to the point where it influences their behavior) by the fact that some people will be hurt by their decisions. In one particularly ambitious study, Dr. Ross Vickers of the U.S. Naval Health Research Center found that effective leaders among Navy enlisted personnel were low on the Trust and Altruism facets. In some circumstances, to be successful one must be somewhat cynical and uncaring.

Clearly, it is possible to be too low on Agreeableness to be a good leader. Someone who scored below the 15th percentile on all six facets could end up being reviled by his or her supervisees and, hence, not very effective. It seems to me that the most effective leaders are agreeable enough so that they have some misgivings about the fact that their decisions will cause pain, but not so many misgivings that they have trouble sleeping at night.

Agreeableness, unlike Neuroticism, for instance, is not a characteristic that is easily changed. Indeed, I have never seen any scientific literature in which mental health professions even tried to help clients become more or less altruistic, or more or less sympathetic. The point is that you have to work with what you have. If you received a low score on this dimension, you probably would not have any interest in becoming a social worker, but you might think hard about entering other helping professions. Physicians, for example, can be found at both ends of this dimension. Low scorers generally gravitate to positions that involve relatively little direct contact with patients, such as surgery or anesthesiology. Those with high scores would probably make good family physicians or pediatricians.

If you had a high score on this dimension, again it is important to recognize your limitations. Be very cautious about getting yourself in a position, such as in management or a business owner, where you have to make decisions that will hurt or displease other people. I am a good example of someone who did not take this advice. Many years ago I was going to make my fortune investing in real estate, but I quickly learned I was too agreeable to be an effective landlord. I hated to evict people even when they clearly deserved evicting, and my ineptitude resulted in my losing a considerable amount of money. Agreeable people can make effective managers, but there will be times when the decisions they are forced to make will torment them.

CHAPTER 23

The Extroversion Scale

The following phrases describe people's behaviors. Use the rating scale below to describe how accurately each statement describes you. Describe yourself as you generally are now, not as you wish to be in the future. Describe yourself as you honestly see yourself in relation to other people you know who are of the same sex and age as you are.

1 = Very Inaccurate
2 = Moderately Inaccurate
3 = Neither Inaccurate nor Accurate
4 = Moderately Accurate
5 = Very Accurate

---

* Adapted from Dr. Lewis R. Goldberg of the Oregon Research Institute.

____ 1. I keep others at a distance.

____ 2. I seek quiet.

____ 3. I take charge.

____ 4. I am always busy.

____ 5. I love excitement.

____ 6. I seldom joke around.

____ 7. I warm up quickly to others.

____ 8. I talk to a lot of different people at parties.

____ 9. I hold back my opinions.

____10. I am always on the go.

____11. I dislike loud music.

____12. I have a lot of fun.

____13. I feel comfortable around people.

____14. I enjoy being part of a group.

____15. I can talk others into doing things.

____16. I do a lot in my spare time.

____17. I would never go hang gliding or bungee jumping.

____18. I express childlike joy.

____19. I act comfortably with others.

____20. I involve others in what I am doing.

____21. I seek to influence others.

____22. I react slowly.

____23. I seek adventure.

____24. I radiate joy.

---

1 = Very Inaccurate; 2 = Moderately Inaccurate;
3 = Neither Inaccurate nor Accurate; 4 = Moderately Accurate;
5 = Very Accurate

____25. I make friends easily.

____26. I love large parties.

____27. I try to lead others.

____28. I let things proceed at their own pace.

____29. I love action.

____30. I am not easily amused.

____31. I cheer people up.

____32. I avoid crowds.

____33. I don't like to draw attention to myself.

____34. I can manage many things at the same time.

____35. I enjoy being part of a loud crowd.

____36. I laugh my way through life.

____37. I am hard to get to know.

____38. I don't like crowded events.

____39. I take control of things.

____40. I like a leisurely lifestyle.

____41. I enjoy being reckless.

____42. I love life.

____43. I often feel uncomfortable around others.

____44. I love surprise parties.

____45. I wait for others to lead the way.

____46. I react quickly.

____47. I act wild and crazy.

____48. I look at the bright side of life.

1 = Very Inaccurate; 2 = Moderately Inaccurate;
3 = Neither Inaccurate nor Accurate; 4 = Moderately Accurate;
5 = Very Accurate

_____49. I avoid contacts with others.

_____50. I prefer to be alone.

_____51. I keep in the background.

_____52. I like to take it easy.

_____53. I am willing to try anything once.

_____54. I laugh aloud.

_____55. I am not really interested in others.

_____56. I want to be left alone.

_____57. I have little to say.

_____58. I like to take my time.

_____59. I seek danger.

_____60. I amuse my friends.

1 = Very Inaccurate; 2 = Moderately Inaccurate;
3 = Neither Inaccurate nor Accurate; 4 = Moderately Accurate;
5 = Very Accurate

SCORING

The Extroversion Scale is comprised of six subscales. The items that appear on each subscale are found below. Items followed by an asterisk (*) are reverse scored.

Friendliness (Fr):	1*, 7, 13, 19, 25, 31, 37*, 43*, 49*, 55*
Gregariousness (Gr):	2*, 8, 14, 20, 26, 32*, 38*, 44, 50*, 56*
Assertiveness (As):	3, 9*, 15, 21, 27, 33*, 39, 45*, 51*, 57*
Activity Level (Al):	4, 10, 16, 22*, 28*, 34, 40*, 46, 52*, 58*
Excitement Seeking (Es):	5, 11*, 17*, 23, 29, 35, 41, 47, 53, 59
Cheerfulness (Ch):	6*, 12, 18, 24, 30*, 36, 42, 48

NORMS

Fr	Gr	As	Al	Es	Ch	Total	Percentile
42	36	38	36	35	40	218	85
37	30	33	31	30	36	192	70
32	24	28	26	24	31	165	50
27	18	23	21	18	26	138	30
22	12	18	16	13	22	112	15

For more information see L. R. Goldberg, "An Alternative 'Description of Personality': The Big-Five Factor Structure," *Journal of Personality and Social Psychology* 59 (1990): 1216–29.

ABOUT THE EXTROVERSION SCALE

Extroversion is the third and one of the more important of the Big Five dimensions. This is a particularly interesting personality characteristic, since almost all of us tend to believe that extroversion is good not only in terms of vocational success but also in our personal and social lives. After all, have you ever heard anyone say something like "You will really like him; he is a real introvert" or "You'll get along well with her; she's not very animated or gregarious." Also, I have never had a client who sought psychotherapy to become less extroverted. I have, on the other hand, had many who wanted to become less introverted.

Despite our positive stereotypes about extroverts and despite the fact that many people wish they were more extroverted, this quality is not always a good thing. True, for many occupations extroversion has been found to be related to success. But you might be surprised to learn that certain facets of extroversion may actually predict poor performance. Let us review the six facets of extroversion and what researchers have learned about how they relate to job performance.

As you might expect, Friendliness, Gregariousness, and Cheerfulness are strongly related to success in the service industry and in sales. Any job that requires one to make cold calls or to interact with new people regularly will be much easier for those whose nature allows them to interact easily with others. This does not mean, however, that low scorers should never consider these types of jobs. I have a friend who is a successful stockbroker despite being quite reserved around people he does not know well. He had always been fascinated with anything having to do with finance and was not about to let his anxiety get in the way of doing something he loved. The first year of his career, his stomach was tied in knots every time he reached for the phone to call a prospective customer. Gradually, he grew more comfortable with the endless rejection, and within a few years he could make cold calls without flinching. Now, twenty years later, he has a solid base of loyal clients but continues to devote several hours each week to cold calling because he finds developing relationships with new clients so gratifying. Low scorers should be warned, however, that like my friend, they will have to be extremely determined if they are to succeed in similar occupations.

Assertiveness is consistently related to success across a variety of occupations. It is important to understand that assertiveness is the socially appropriate expression of one's thoughts and feelings. Assertive people are able to stand up for themselves; they are able to get their point of view across. Assertive people are not, however, obnoxious or overbearing. If you received a high score on this facet, you are fortunate to possess a quality that almost without exception, employers are looking for.

If you received a low score, the good news is that with a little effort you can become more assertive. Workshops designed to help people such as yourself are relatively common (you may want to try your college counseling center or state employment agency), and they are generally quite effective. If you cannot find a work-shop, most mental health professionals are familiar with the techniques of assertiveness training. If you did score below the 50th per-centile, it would be worth your while to try to become more assertive. The odds are strong that such a change would help you to perform better on your job and, perhaps just as importantly, help you to communicate your effectiveness to your colleagues and supervisors. I have known nonassertive peo-ple who were quite competent at their jobs but never received the recognition they deserved because it was so difficult for them to let others know of their accomplishments.

High scorers on the Activity Level facet are doers; they abhor the idea that any grass might grow under their feet. These people are more successful than their low-scoring peers simply because they make more of an effort. Their need to be busy means that instead of vegetating in front of the television on Saturday after-noon, they might read trade publications or learn a new software program—any-thing to improve their skills and make them more valuable to their employers.

I can sympathize with those of you who received low scores, since I have the same natural inclination. I have found that the best way for me to increase my activity level is to find a project that interests me. So, if you scored below the 50th percentile, you do not necessarily need to rely on your will power to get off your duff; you may simply need to develop plans that get you excited. Once you do that, your activity level should take care of itself.

If extroverts have a dark side, it is related to the Excitement Seeking dimen-sion. This quality can be good; high scor-ers are not afraid to try new things or to take a calculated risk. A majority of people who quit secure jobs to start their own businesses are high on this facet. But high scorers are also likely to get into trouble as a result of their craving for novel experi-ences. They are more likely than their low-scoring colleagues to experiment with drugs or to develop problems with alco-hol. They are also prone to get themselves into awkward positions as a result of their interest in having novel sexual experi-ences. (Could Clinton be an excitement seeker?) Although there are more reasons for employers to look for extroverted applicants than not, there are a handful of published studies that provide justifica-tion for avoiding them. If you received a high score on this scale, you would be wise to monitor your intake of mind-altering substances very carefully.

While the evidence that extroversion is related to job success is sufficiently clear to convince employers to look for this quality in their applicants, I believe that over time, people who score in the middle ranges of these six facets make the most valued employees. It is hard to beat the extremely extroverted person when it comes to making a good first impression, but these people can become tiresome. They often feel that they have to make a contribution to every discussion regard-less of whether they have anything to say, and they tend to be less sensitive to the feelings of those around them. Extrover-sion can be a good thing, but it is easy to overdo it—at least from the perspective of an introvert.

CHAPTER 24

The Openness to Experience Scale

The following phrases describe people's behaviors. Use the rating scale below to describe how accurately each statement describes you. Describe yourself as you generally are now, not as you wish to be in the future. Describe yourself as you honestly see yourself in relation to other people you know who are of the same sex and age as you are.

1 = Very Inaccurate
2 = Moderately Inaccurate
3 = Neither Inaccurate nor Accurate
4 = Moderately Accurate
5 = Very Accurate

* Adapted from Dr. Lewis Goldberg of the Oregon Research Institute.

_____ 1. I have a vivid imagination.

_____ 2. I do not enjoy watching dance performances.

_____ 3. I don't understand people who get emotional.

_____ 4. I am attached to conventional ways.

_____ 5. I avoid difficult reading material.

_____ 6. I like to stand during the national anthem.

_____ 7. I have difficulty imagining things.

_____ 8. I believe in the importance of art.

_____ 9. I experience very few emotional highs and lows.

_____10. I prefer variety to routine.

_____11. I like to solve complex problems

_____12. I believe that we should be tough on crime.

_____13. I enjoy wild flights of fantasy.

_____14. I like music.

_____15. I rarely notice my emotional reactions.

_____16. I like to visit new places.

_____17. I love to read challenging material.

_____18. I tend to vote for liberal political candidates.

_____19. I love to daydream.

_____20. I see beauty in things that others might not notice.

_____21. I experience my emotions intensely.

_____22. I am interested in many things.

_____23. I have a rich vocabulary.

_____24. I believe that there is no absolute right or wrong.

1 = Very Inaccurate; 2 = Moderately Inaccurate;
3 = Neither Inaccurate nor Accurate; 4 = Moderately Accurate;
5 = Very Accurate

_____25. I seldom get lost in thought.

_____26. I do not like concerts.

_____27. I am not easily affected by my emotions.

_____28. I dislike new foods.

_____29. I am not interested in theoretical discussions.

_____30. I believe that we coddle criminals too much.

_____31. I do not have a good imagination.

_____32. I do not enjoy going to art museums.

_____33. I seldom get emotional.

_____34. I am a creature of habit.

_____35. I can handle a lot of information.

_____36. I believe that criminals should receive help rather than punishment.

_____37. I like to get lost in thought.

_____38. I love flowers.

_____39. I feel others' emotions.

_____40. I don't like the idea of change.

_____41. I have difficulty understanding abstract ideas.

_____42. I believe laws should be strictly enforced.

_____43. I seldom daydream.

_____44. I do not like poetry.

_____45. I am passionate about causes.

_____46. I like to begin new things.

_____47. I avoid philosophical discussions.

_____48. I believe that too much tax money goes to support artists.

1 = Very Inaccurate; 2 = Moderately Inaccurate;
3 = Neither Inaccurate nor Accurate; 4 = Moderately Accurate;
5 = Very Accurate

____49. I indulge in my fantasies.

____50. I enjoy the beauty of nature.

____51. I enjoy examining myself and my life.

____52. I prefer to stick with things that I know.

____53. I enjoy thinking about things.

____54. I believe in one true religion.

____55. I spend time reflecting on things.

____56. I do not like art.

____57. I try to understand myself.

____58. I dislike changes.

____59. I am not interested in abstract ideas.

____60. I tend to vote for conservative political candidates.

1 = Very Inaccurate; 2 = Moderately Inaccurate;
3 = Neither Inaccurate nor Accurate; 4 = Moderately Accurate;
5 = Very Accurate

SCORING

The Openness to Experience Scale is comprised of six subscales. The items appearing on each subscale appear below. Items marked with an asterisk (*) are reverse scored.

Imagination (Im):	1, 7*, 13, 19, 25*, 31*, 37, 43*, 49, 55
Artistic Interests (Ai):	2*, 8, 14, 20, 26*, 32*, 38, 44*, 50, 56*
Emotionality (Em):	3*, 9*, 15*, 21, 27*, 33*, 39, 45, 51, 57
Adventurousness (Ad):	4*, 10, 16, 22, 28*, 34*, 40*, 46, 52*, 58
Intellect (In):	5*, 11, 17, 23, 29*, 35, 41*, 47*, 53, 59*
Liberalism (Li):	6*, 12*, 18, 24, 30*, 36, 42*, 48*, 54*, 60*

NORMS

Im	Ai	Em	Ad	In	Li	Total	Percentile
41	46	42	39	42	32	240	85
36	41	37	34	37	26	208	70
30	36	31	29	31	19	175	50
24	31	25	24	25	12	142	30
19	26	20	19	20	10	110	15

For more information see L. R. Goldberg, "An Alternative 'Description of Personality': The Big-Five Factor Structure," *Journal of Personality and Social Psychology* 59 (1990): 1216–29.

ABOUT THE OPENNESS TO EXPERIENCE SCALE

The fourth dimension of the Big Five, Openness to Experience, has received less attention than the others by personnel psychologists. There are several studies that demonstrate it can be a useful selection instrument, but at present the evidence suggests that it is not as powerful a predictor as the other four dimensions; hence it has been relatively neglected by researchers. I suspect, though, that this will change over the next few years. There is a strong theoretical basis for believing that this scale is related to success in a number of occupations. Let us review what is known (and what I suspect) about the facets that make up Openness to Experience.

People high in Imagination find it easy to get lost in their thoughts. This quality is closely related to creativity, and high scorers are the ones who are likely to make important contributions to art, literature, and technological innovation. Low scorers may be better at getting the nitty-gritty work done, but it is the high scorers that are likely to come up with the new ideas that makes this nitty-gritty work easier or more productive.

The meaning of Artistic Interests is straightforward. People who receive high scores on this facet will enjoy occupations that allow them to express these interests. Musicians, artists, and actors are obviously high scorers, but commercial artists, graphic designers, and teachers have opportunities to express their artistic side as well.

People who score high on Emotionality tend to experience and express their emotions more intensely than most people. There is virtually no research to suggest that this is either a positive or negative predictor of success in any occupation. I suspect, though, that it is inversely related to another characteristic that employers look for—resistance to stress. It seems logical that people who experience intense emotions would have strong reactions to stressful working environments and, consequently, would be less effective under such circumstances.

Adventurousness characterizes people who love the new and the different. Routines are an anathema to them; they look forward to a variety of challenges. If you received a high score on this facet, obviously you should avoid occupations that involve repetitive duties. You should keep in mind that job repetition is independent of job status. I know several unhappy physicians and attorneys who were attracted to their fields because they appeared to offer the opportunity to continually expand their horizons. But the reality of checking countless sore throats or going from one real estate closing to the next can be deadly to the adventurous. On the other hand, I know adventurous carpenters and mechanics who love their jobs because each project presents a new set of challenges.

People who receive high scores on the Intellect facet, as you might expect, place a high value on the intellectual aspects of life. While it is possible for people who are, at best, average in intelligence to receive high scores on this facet, as a group high scorers are more intelligent than low scorers. Most of us are reasonably accurate judges of our intelligence, so people who say they have a rich vocabulary (item 23) or are able to handle a lot of information (35) probably would receive high scores on a test of intelligence—such as the Cognitive Ability Test in chapter 19. If you are both intelligent and high in Intellect, it is important that you work in an occupation that presents you with challenges. You will not be satisfied with less.

The meaning of Liberalism is straightforward. High scorers occupy the left side of the political spectrum, and low scorers can be found on the right. Personnel psychologists have not gathered evidence as to whether this facet predicts success in any occupations, but we do know that certain occupations tend to attract liberals while others attract conservatives. The helping professions, teachers, college professors, and government employees are among those who voted heavily for Clinton during the 1996 election; people in business and finance were likely to support Dole. While it is clearly the case that one's political leanings are related to one's vocational interests, I know of no reason to believe that a conservative could not be a happy and effective social worker or that a liberal could not be a happy and effective stockbroker.

As you can tell from the above, work with the Openness to Experience dimension is, for the most part, still in the early, speculative stages. There are, however, two well-established findings. First, Openness to Experience is related to successfully completing training programs. It makes sense that trainers would find high scorers more malleable. They would be open to learning new approaches or new methods. Low scorers, on the other hand, tend to be resistant to anything other than the tried and true. They are likely to be suspicious of anything that smacks of innovation. Second, Openness to Experience is related to risk taking. So, people who receive high scores on this scale are more likely to start their own businesses than are low scorers.

The six facets that make up Openness to Experience reflect one's values as much as one's personality. This suggests that unlike the characteristics measured by the other four dimensions of the Big Five, most people are not interested in changing their values. And indeed, they would find it quite difficult to do so even if they tried. I know I've experienced a complete lack of success in developing an appreciation for the artistic, despite repeated urging from several friends. So this is a "work with what you've got" situation. Because you are unlikely to be able to change your level of Openness to Experience, the most fruitful approach is to find an occupation that allows you the opportunity to express your particular values.

CHAPTER 25

The Conscientiousness Scale

The following phrases describe people's behaviors, attitudes, and feelings. Use the rating scale below to describe how accurately each statement describes you. Describe yourself as you generally are now, not as you wish to be in the future. Describe yourself as you honestly see yourself in relation to other people you know who are of the same sex and age as you are.

1 = Very Inaccurate
2 = Moderately Inaccurate
3 = Neither Inaccurate nor Accurate
4 = Moderately Accurate
5 = Very Accurate

* Adapted from Dr. Lewis R. Goldberg of the Oregon Research Institute.

_____ 1. I complete tasks successfully.

_____ 2. I am not bothered by disorder.

_____ 3. I try to follow the rules.

_____ 4. I go straight for the goal.

_____ 5. I postpone decisions.

_____ 6. I often make last-minute plans.

_____ 7. I excel in what I do.

_____ 8. I like order.

_____ 9. I keep my promises.

_____10. I work hard.

_____11. I get chores done right away.

_____12. I avoid mistakes.

_____13. I don't see the consequences of things.

_____14. I like to tidy up.

_____15. I pay my bills on time.

_____16. I turn plans into actions.

_____17. I have difficulty starting tasks.

_____18. I act without thinking.

_____19. I handle tasks smoothly.

_____20. I want everything to be "just right."

_____21. I tell the truth.

_____22. I plunge into tasks with all my heart.

_____23. I am always prepared.

_____24. I choose my words with care.

1 = Very Inaccurate; 2 = Moderately Inaccurate;
3 = Neither Inaccurate nor Accurate; 4 = Moderately Accurate;
5 = Very Accurate

_____25. I have little to contribute.

_____26. I love order and regularity.

_____27. I listen to my conscience.

_____28. I do more than what's expected of me.

_____29. I need a push to get started.

_____30. I do crazy things.

_____31. I don't understand things.

_____32. I am not bothered by messy people.

_____33. I misrepresent the facts.

_____34. I put little time and effort into my work.

_____35. I waste my time.

_____36. I rush into things.

_____37. I am sure of my ground.

_____38. I leave my belongings around.

_____39. I break rules.

_____40. I set high standards for myself and others.

_____41. I start tasks right away.

_____42. I stick to my chosen path.

_____43. I come up with good solutions.

_____44. I leave a mess in my room.

_____45. I break my promises.

_____46. I do just enough work to get by.

_____47. I find it difficult to get down to work.

_____48. I jump into things without thinking.

---

1 = Very Inaccurate; 2 = Moderately Inaccurate;
3 = Neither Inaccurate nor Accurate; 4 = Moderately Accurate;
5 = Very Accurate

____49. I know how to get things done.

____50. I do things according to a plan.

____51. I get others to do my duties.

____52. I demand quality.

____53. I get to work at once.

____54. I make rash decisions.

____55. I misjudge situations.

____56. I often forget to put things back in their proper place.

____57. I do the opposite of what is asked.

____58. I am not highly motivated to succeed.

____59. I carry out my plans.

____60. I like to act on a whim.

1 = Very Inaccurate; 2 = Moderately Inaccurate;
3 = Neither Inaccurate nor Accurate; 4 = Moderately Accurate;
5 = Very Accurate

SCORING

The Conscientiousness Scale is comprised of six subscales. The items that appear on each subscale are found below. Items followed by an asterisk (*) are reverse scored.

Self-efficacy (Se):	1, 7, 13*, 19, 25*, 31*, 37, 43, 49, 55*
Orderliness (Or):	2*, 8, 14, 20, 26, 32*, 38*, 44*, 50, 56*
Dutifulness (Du):	3, 9, 15, 21, 27, 33*, 39*, 45*, 51*, 57*
Achievement-Striving (As):	4, 10, 16, 22, 28, 34*, 40, 46*, 52, 58*
Self-discipline (Sd):	5*, 11, 17*, 23, 29*, 35*, 41, 47*, 53, 59
Cautiousness (Ca):	6*, 12, 18*, 24, 30*, 36*, 42, 48*, 54*, 60*

NORMS

Se	Or	Du	As	Sd	Ca	Total	Percentile
44	43	48	46	42	39	261	85
40	38	44	42	37	34	233	70
36	32	39	37	31	29	205	50
32	26	34	32	26	24	177	30
28	21	30	28	21	19	145	15

For more information see L. R. Goldberg, "An Alternative 'Description of Personality': The Big-Five Factor Structure," *Journal of Personality and Social Psychology* 59 (1990): 1216–29.

ABOUT THE CONSCIENTIOUSNESS SCALE

The Conscientiousness Scale represents one of the most widely used types of tests in employment settings. Recall that in chapter 20 we talked about two categories of integrity tests. The test in chapter 20 is an example of what is called an overt integrity test. The Conscientiousness Scale is an example of the second category, the personality-based integrity test. These tests came into use during the late 1980s, after the use of the polygraph, or lie detector, was made illegal in pre-employment screening. Both overt and personality-based integrity tests have been extensively researched, and a majority of personnel psychologists have concluded that they are second only to tests of cognitive ability in their power to provide useful information about potential employees. Virtually all employers are eager to hire applicants with high scores on this type of test. Let us review the meaning of the scores on the six facets of this Conscientiousness Scale.

People who score high on Self-efficacy, the first facet of the Conscientiousness Scale, take pride in their work. It is important to their self-esteem that they perform their duties in a competent fashion, and they will do what it takes to get the job done. High scorers can be trusted to do a good job even if they receive minimal supervision, since their motivation comes from within. Low scorers, on the other hand, must be closely supervised if they are to perform their duties in a competent

fashion, since they derive little satisfaction from a job well done. They tend to see their jobs as an onerous duty, and their goal is to expend as little effort as possible and still keep their positions.

The Orderliness facet is more important to some employers than others. A high degree of Orderliness would be desirable for many positions, such as for accountants, administrative assistants, and scheduling clerks, but it is irrelevant for others. Judging from the appearance of my office, as well as those of several of my colleagues, orderliness is probably not related to success in many occupations.

Dutifulness is one of the more important facets. It is related to a category of behaviors called job delinquency. These include employee theft, substance abuse on the job, absenteeism, and arguments with and even assaults on coworkers and supervisors. Job delinquency costs business billions of dollars each year, so many employers will not consider applicants who score below the mean on tests similar to this one.

Achievement-Striving overlaps a good deal with Self-efficacy, but it tends to identify people who are especially interested in moving up the occupational ladder. Like those high in Self-efficacy, high scorers on the Achievement-Striving Scale derive satisfaction from doing their jobs well, but they also work hard and diligently because they have an eye on that possible promotion. Employers often are looking for applicants who are high in Achievement-Striving, but not always. I consult for a company, for instance, that likes to hire office workers who are high in Self-efficacy but only average in Achievement-Striving. Because these positions offer little opportunity for advancement, they believe that applicants who are too ambitious will quickly become dissatisfied with their jobs. This same company, on the other hand, loves to find applicants high in Achievement-Striving when they are hiring sales representatives. As long as these people retain their integrity, they cannot be too ambitious.

Self-discipline is an essential ingredient for virtually all successful employees. High scorers have the ability to plod ahead and to make steady progress, even when they are faced with an unpleasant task or when their motivation is at a low ebb. Employers can be confident that high scorers will get the job done even when they are not being closely supervised.

Cautiousness is also a valued characteristic because people who receive high scores on this facet are unlikely to engage in impulsive behavior that is likely to be costly to the company. Cautious employees consider the potential consequences of their actions. They are not likely to make an off-hand remark that could result in the loss of a valued customer or a hasty decision that could harm the company's reputation. Cautiousness does not imply a reluctance to take risks, by the way. Cautious people can be risk takers, but they carefully consider all the options before making the decision. They are not averse to taking chances, but they want to ensure that as much as possible, they stack the deck in their favor before playing their hand.

The psychological literature suggests that about half of all applicants who take tests such as the Conscientiousness Scale are labeled as unsuitable. So, if you scored above the 50th percentile, you probably have little cause to be concerned about such tests.

If you scored below the 50th percentile, your most adaptive strategy would be to think hard about your shortcomings and devise a plan to rectify them. It is true that such tests are susceptible to faking, and the odds are good that with practice and determination you could "fool" the test. But fooling the test will do little for you in the long run. Unless you change your approach to the world of work, your employer is likely to discover your true nature eventually, and you will once again have to face the task of job hunting. Your best chance of having a long and satisfying career is by endeavoring to become the type of worker that employers value. They are willing to pay well for the very best.

Translating Knowledge into Action

Now that you have completed all the tests in this book, you should have a much clearer idea about your strengths as well as your weaknesses. I also hope that you have a clearer idea about what it takes to find the right career for you, a career that you will find highly gratifying. And finally, I hope you feel better prepared to go out there, get that all-important invitation for an interview, and knock 'em dead with your ability to present yourself well.

The most important point to remember is that knowledge is not enough. No matter how much you may have learned about yourself and the employment selection process from this book, it will be of little value unless you translate your knowledge into action. This book should be the starting point in your search for the right career, not the culmination of it. Follow through on the suggestions I made in the various chapters. Go to the library and browse through the various reference books. Search the Internet for the Web sites of professional organizations and companies that interest you. Begin to make appointments to talk with people who are working in the fields that you are considering. Make a list of the steps you must take to obtain the qualifications you need for your career. Consider how you can best communicate your strengths to potential employers. And perhaps most important of all, articulate a plan for dealing with any weaknesses that you identified through these tests. Be active, be bold, and go after what you want. The meek may inherit the earth, but they won't find the best jobs.

For a majority of you, I suspect that the most useful role of these tests is that they articulated what you have always suspected. I doubt, for instance, that there are any quiet, retiring people whose dreams of a career in sales were dashed when they found they had a low score on the Extroversion Scale. And men and women who have a history of failing to complete assignments in a timely fashion were unlikely to be surprised that their score on the Procrastination Scale indicated that they need to make some changes if they are to have a successful career.

If, however, you are one of the minority who was surprised by some of your scores, it is important to keep in mind that psychological tests are far from perfect instruments. They can be used to make accurate predictions about groups of people, but they do not do as well when they are used to make predictions about individuals. So, if you are disturbed by one or more of your scores, I would recommend that you think hard about your situation; but I would strongly recommend against making a change in your career plans based upon a single test score. To illustrate, if you have always imagined becoming a research scientist and winning the Nobel Prize, you should not abandon your dreams simply because you obtained a low score on the Creativity Scale or the Openness Scale. Yes, low scores on these scales may suggest that your plans will not unfold as easily as they might if you received high scores, but low scores by no means preclude the possibility of success. I honestly believe that with determination and diligence, most people can overcome any obstacles in order to accomplish their goals.

Finally, I hope you enjoyed taking these tests as much as I enjoyed putting them together for you. The process of self-discovery can be exciting, and I will feel gratified if I helped to provide you with the impetus to go out there and get what you want.

ABOUT THE AUTHOR

LOUIS JANDA, PH.D. is a professor of psychology at Old Dominion University in Norfolk, Virginia and a practicing clinical psychologist. His practice includes psychological testing for private business and industry. He is also the author of *The Psychologist's Book of Self-Tests* and *Love & Sex Tests*.